UNLOCKING
THE PURPOSE
IN YOU

JOHN STANKO

UrbanPress
PUBLISHING YOUR DREAMS

Unlocking the Purpose In You
by John W. Stanko
Copyright ©2025 John W. Stanko

Unless otherwise identified, Scripture quotations are taken from THE HOLY BIBLE: New International Version ©1978 by the New York International Bible Society, used by permission of Zondervan Bible Publishers.

Unless otherwise identified, Scripture taken from the HOLY BIBLE, NEW INTERNATIONAL VERSION®. Copyright © 1973, 1978, 1984 by International Bible Society. Used by permission of Zondervan Publishing House. All rights reserved.

Scripture quotations marked NASB are taken from the Holy Bible, New American Standard Bible, copyright © 1960, 1971, 1977, 1995, 2020 by The Lockman Foundation. All rights reserved.

Scriptures marked AMP are taken from The Amplified Bible, Old Testament. Copyright 1965, 1987, by The Zondervan Corporation.

Scriptures marked MSG are taken from THE MESSAGE. Copyright © by Eugene H. Peterson 1993, 1994, 1995, 1996, 2000, 2002. Used by permission of NavPress Publishing Group.

Scriptures marked NAS are taken from the New American Standard Bible, Copyright ©1960, 1962, 1963, 1968, 1971, 1973, 1975, 1977 by The Lockman Foundation.

Scripture marked NKJ are taken from the New King James Version. Copyright © 1982 by Thomas Nelson, Inc. Scripture marked NLT are taken from the Holy Bible, New Living Translation, copyright ©1996. Used by permission of Tyndale House Publishers, Inc., Wheaton IL 60189.

Scripture marked TLB are taken from The Living Bible by Kenneth N. Taylor, Used by permission of Tyndale House, Wheaton, IL. All are used by permission. All rights reserved.

ISBN 978-1-63360-316-5

For Worldwide Distribution
Printed in the U.S.A.

Urban Press
P.O. Box 8881
Pittsburgh, PA 15221-0881
412.646.2780

TABLE OF CONTENTS

Section One - Unlocking the Power of Your Purpose

End Notes

Section Two - Unlocking the Power of You

INTRODUCTION

Welcome to this special combined volume of two of my most impactful and widely received books in the Unlocking series: *Unlocking the Power of Your Purpose* and *Unlocking the Power of You*. Over the years, both books have touched the lives of thousands of readers across the globe and have consistently ranked as the best-selling titles in the series. It's for that reason—and because their messages are so closely connected—that I've brought them together into one volume with two distinct but complementary sections.

The first section, *Unlocking the Power of Your Purpose*, is rooted in a simple yet profound truth: if God wants you to do His will, then He must reveal what that will is. This book helps readers discover, clarify, and live out their God-given purpose. Born out of my *Monday Memo* email series that has encouraged believers weekly for more than two decades, this section presents 52 purpose-based reflections, principles, and personal stories designed to help you navigate your quest for purpose with clarity and faith.

The second section, *Unlocking the Power of You*, shifts the focus inward. Many people mistakenly believe they must become someone else—more disciplined, more outgoing, less flawed—before God can use them. This part of the book counters that myth with a liberating truth: God is ready to work through who you are, right now. Through real-life coaching stories and practical insight, this section will help you embrace your personality, stop fighting yourself, and release the inherent power in how God made you.

Together, these two sections provide a holistic roadmap to help you discover who you are and why you're here. My prayer is that as you read, reflect, and apply what you learn, you will find the confidence to live out your unique calling with courage and joy.

Let the unlocking begin.

John W. Stanko
Pittsburgh, Pennsylvania
July 2025

UNLOCKING
THE POWER
OF
YOUR PURPOSE

STUDY #1
NEW PERSPECTIVES ON PURPOSE

I receive a lot of questions when I lecture on the topic of purpose. Over the years, the questions asked most often, along with my answers, have been as follows:

Q. CAN MY PURPOSE CHANGE OVER TIME?

A. No. How you fulfill your purpose may change, but your purpose remains the same. I have fulfilled my purpose, which is to create order out of chaos in a few different job roles. My purpose is the same; how I do it may change.

Q. CAN I HAVE MORE THAN ONE PURPOSE?

A. No. You can have many gifts and talents, or different ways to express or fulfill your purpose, but your purpose is a clear, simple, and singular summary of your essence.

Q. SHOULD OR IS IT POSSIBLE FOR A HUSBAND AND WIFE TO HAVE THE SAME PURPOSE?

A. No. While it is possible for a couple to have the same purpose, I have found it to be rare. Even if both work in the same business, mission or ministry, each partner will have a different purpose and function in that same organization. Usually, those purposes complement one another.

Q. WHAT IS THE DIFFERENCE BETWEEN A GIFT AND PURPOSE?

A. A gift is like a tool that you carry with you to help fulfill your purpose. A plumber's purpose is not to "wrench." The wrench helps the plumber achieve his or her purpose to repair or build. Your gifts do the same for you, but they are not to be confused with your purpose.

Q. WHAT IS THE DIFFERENCE BETWEEN MINISTRY AND PURPOSE?

A. Too often, we are tempted to separate what we do in church from what we do outside of church. We tend to think of ministry as related to church work, and purpose as something that may or may not fit into our church role. I contend that there is no difference between the two.

I met with a man in Atlanta who had a career in human resources. It was clear to me, however, that he was functioning as a pastor to many people. When I suggested that perhaps he was a chaplain or pastor in his company, he rejected the idea at first because he didn't have a pulpit or even enjoy public speaking. Yet he had clearly cared for and been a shepherd to people during his entire corporate career.

By the end of our meeting, he began to see his purpose was to care for people in a business setting. He saw that his purpose was his ministry; it just wasn't taking place within the walls of a church building. That knowledge set him free to be who God made him to be and freed him from thinking his ministry and purpose were two different things.

Perhaps you aren't clear about your purpose because you have put God in a box. Maybe you are a prophet, but everyone knows that prophets only function in a church setting. Who said that? You bring healing and wholeness to people but never lay hands on anyone or do it within a church. Does that limit your purpose or usefulness to God? Are you a preacher, but your pulpit is in a school or hospital? I met a man once whose title was school principal or headmaster, but whose purpose was to pastor the children who attended his school, and to pastor their parents as well.

The following words of Robert K. Greenleaf can help set you free to minister (which simply means to serve) in whatever setting the Lord chooses for you, whether it's inside or outside the church:

> The great religious prophets of the future will not necessarily be theologians, philosophers, or people of literature. They are as likely to be lawyers, doctors, businesspeople, scientists, or politicians, and they will carry out their prophetic roles while functioning at a high level of excellence in their professional field. In fact, unless significant prophecy emerges in all these places, the vision, without which the people perish, will not be sufficiently evident.
>
> The world society in which we are all inextricably involved is far too complex, it is in too revolutionary a mood, and it is fast becoming too literate and aware of its sources of expertise for very much of the prophetic wisdom it needs to be uttered by ministers, scholars, or writers. These people will, of course, continue to serve, but more on a par with those who are more immersed in the ongoing work of the world.
>
> Businesses, government bureaus, law firms, clinics, and scientific laboratories have not only become large, sophisticated institutions and important sources of new knowledge, but are just as likely to harbor a philosopher, a prophet, or a saint as is the monastery or the university.[1]

STUDY #2
I FOUND MINE IN A BOOK

I once met a man named Michael who had read all my books. The church he attended was started in part because the founders had read my purpose message. At the time of our meeting, Michael was working for the church. When I asked him what his purpose was, he said, "I'm not sure." So I did what I always do: I began asking questions.

It didn't take long for me to hear some key words: music, excellence, and projects were a few of them. Then one phrase stood out. He said, "I like to make things sing." What a colorful phrase! He wasn't saying that everything had to be musical, though. "Making everything sing" stated his commitment to excellence in whatever he did. He didn't want things to "hum" or "whistle;" he wanted every project, whether musical or not, to be the best expression of its unique purpose. I left Michael to consider whether his life purpose is to make things sing.

I receive many inquiries from people needing help finding their purpose. It recently occurred to me that I found my purpose—to create order out of chaos—when I had read those words in a book. They "jumped out" at me, and I have never been the same since. I thought I would provide some phrases for you to study to see if the same thing would happen to you.

I found the list below in a book entitled, *Whistle While*

You Work: Heeding Your Life's Calling, by Richard Leider and David A. Shapiro. The authors refer to this as a list of "Calling Cards"—a concept they developed to help people like you and me find our life's calling and purpose. They explain:

> Each of these callings describes a core gift. Each calling comes directly from someone's experience. We have been collecting callings in seminars, workshops, and coaching sessions with individuals and groups from all walks of life. The list of 52 callings we have come up with represents the "essence of essences" in our research. (This doesn't mean that there are not callings other than our 52; it does, however, mean that these 52 represent those that have best withstood real-world testing.)[2]

I am including half of their list in this study; you will find the other half in the following one. Read both lists and see if anything stirs you. Feel free to focus on one of these phrases that seems to be a close description of who you are. Allow God to "energize" that statement and make it your own or modify it in some way to make it a better fit for you. I hope the Lord will do for you what He did for me: by taking someone else's words, I was able to define my purpose. I hope that you can do the same thing. Happy seeking!

LIST OF CALLING CARDS

CATEGORY ONE: REALISTIC

Building Things
Fixing Things
Growing Things
Making Things Work
Shaping Environments
Solving Problems

CATEGORY TWO: CONVENTIONAL

Straightening Things Up
Doing the Numbers
Getting Things Right
Operating Things
Organizing Things
Processing Things

CATEGORY THREE: INVESTIGATIVE

Advancing Ideas
Investigating Things
Analyzing Information
Researching Things
Putting the Pieces Together
Translating Things
Getting to the Heart of Matters

STUDY #3
PANNING FOR GOLD

.

I suppose that if I had lived in Alaska, my first book would have been titled *Life is a Goldmine: Can You Pan It?* as opposed to *Can You Dig It?* The early Alaskan settlers panned for gold in Alaska's streams and rivers in hopes of finding their golden treasure. With that in mind, I decided to try my hand at gold panning one time while on an Alaskan cruise.

I did indeed find about ten small pieces of gold during my panning experience. Digging or panning for gold is like what you and I go through to find our life purpose. How so? consider these similarities:

1. *You can pan on your own, but having someone who knows how to do it is a great help.* My guide Tom had begun panning two years earlier. He taught us the proper procedures that enabled each one of us to find gold. When you are looking for your purpose, it often helps to involve other people. Ask them what they think your purpose may be. Better yet, find someone who knows their purpose and ask them to help you find yours.

2. *Panning is hard work.* As I stood over a trough, panning for the gold I found, my back began to ache. I thought about those who panned in the cold Alaskan weather, standing in cold water, and bending over for most of the day. Finding your purpose can be hard work, too,

and there is no guarantee when you'll find it or what you'll go through to discover the big golden nugget awaiting you.

3. *You don't need a lot of tools.* You only need a pan to discover gold, not a lot of sophisticated equipment. As you search for your purpose, you start where you are, with what you have, and look around you in faith.

4. *You can't see the gold right away.* When I began, my pan was filled with dirt and gravel. When you search for your purpose; you can't see the "gold" because of all the other "stuff" in your life. It's there, however, and you must know how to find it.

5. *It's exciting when you find the gold.* When I found the gold at the bottom of my pan, I felt like I was rich! When you find your life purpose, you feel the same way. The God of the universe knows who you are, and He gave you something to do that's just right for you.

6. *The gold stays in the pan.* Gold is so heavy that it's almost impossible to lose it when you're panning. Your life purpose is the same way; it's a part of you that goes with you wherever you are and is relevant no matter what mistakes you've made.

In the previous study, I promised to give you the second half of the "Calling Cards" from the book entitled, *Whistle While You Work: Heeding Your Life's Calling,* by Richard Leider and David A. Shapiro.[3]

So are you ready to pan for gold? Put these calling cards in your pan and swirl them around to see if any stay in the bottom as the gold of your life. If you're not sure, then keep swirling them around in your mind and heart. Keep looking, and I promise that you'll find the riches that lie in all the "stuff" in your life.

CATEGORY FOUR: ENTERPRISING

Bringing Out Potential

Exploring the Way

Managing Things
Persuading People
StartingThings
Selling Intangibles
Opening Doors
Empowering Others

CATEGORY FIVE: SOCIAL

Awakening Spirit
Bringing Joy
Building Relationships
Creating Dialogue
Creating Trust
Facilitating Change
Getting Participation
Giving Care
Healing Wounds
Helping Overcome Obstacles
Instructing People
Resolving Disputes

CATEGORY SIX: ARTISTIC

Adding Humor
Breaking Molds
Creating Things
Composing Things
Designing Things
Moving Through Space
Performing Events
Seeing Possibilities
Seeing the Big Picture
Writing Things

STUDY #4
WHAT'S IN A NAME?

My encounter with Dennis is one of my favorite PurposeQuest stories. Dennis attended a seminar in Virginia a few years ago and was not impressed with my message. In fact, he politely but firmly opposed it as a "management fad" that was not to be found in the Bible. I urged him to be patient until I reached the end of the seminar, but he found it hard to do so. He just wasn't buying what I said.

After the session, Dennis came to me and reiterated his disagreement with my conclusions. He felt that my purpose message was too subjective and open to misinterpretation. He then issued his plea: "I challenge you to find any theme of purpose in the diverse activities I have been involved with in my lifetime." Intrigued by his challenge, I accepted.

As he went through his list of seemingly unrelated activities, I started to regret that I had agreed to the challenge. Then I saw something that gave me hope. "It seems to me," I said, "that the common theme here is not *what* you've done, but *why* you've done it. Isn't it true that you've been called on to do all those things because they weren't quite what they could be?" I closed with the statement, "It seems to me that you were born to bring a measure of excellence to whatever the Lord wants you to do."

Dennis still wasn't impressed and left, only to return the next day for the rest of my seminar. This time he shared an exciting revelation he had the night before. He told the class that after he left the previous meeting, he had been reminded of the literal meaning of his name "Dennis" in Greek. Dennis means "discerner of excellence," and this man had suddenly come face to face with a very dramatic understanding of who he was and what he was born to do.

I wish all PurposeQuests ended so well and neatly, but they don't. Some people search and search and become discouraged in the process. Others settle for half answers, and still others for pat answers that lack personal meaning and application. Where do you fit in?

I want to suggest a few more guidelines for finding your purpose. Consider these issues if you are still searching or helping someone who is.

1. *Your purpose may not be found in what you're doing, but rather in why you're doing it.* That was the case with Dennis. He brought excellence to non-excellent performance by doing many different things. In trying to find his purpose, he was focusing on the wrong thing.

2. *Your purpose may be defined by who you're not.* You will often go where you are least comfortable to fulfill your purpose. My purpose is to create order out of chaos. I love order but always find myself, at least for a while, in chaos. The very thing I'm not (chaotic) gives expression to the very thing I am (ordered).

3. *Your purpose may be expressed in many ways.* I create order out of chaos, but I've done it as a writer, pastor, consultant, teacher, and administrator. I've been involved in many activities, but there has always been one common purpose and theme.

4. *Often your purpose is as close as the name your parents gave you,* only you can't see it. God can open your eyes, however, to see what you couldn't previously see. I trust that this will soon be the experience either for you or someone you're helping. Are there any clues in your name or nickname that can help you find your purpose?

STUDY #5
FRUIT AND PURPOSE

I've never looked for a job in my life. Every job I've had has come looking for me. And each job has needed what I had to offer: a life purpose of creating order out of chaos and potential.

As I was sitting on the beach one day in Hilton Head Island, South Carolina, I was thinking about what Jesus said: "By their fruit you will know them." What fruit or results are you known for? If you can answer that, you're well on your way to knowing your life purpose.

I'm known as someone who can bring order out of a mess. I see the potential in people and situations that others can't see. It's not what I hope to do or produce. It's the fruit that I was born to produce; it's the real me.

A friend sent me an article entitled, "Are You Listening to Your Life?" by Parker Palmer. I want to quote it to help you "listen" for the fruit that you're known for:

> Vocation doesn't come from a voice "out there" calling me to become something I'm not. It comes from a voice "in here" calling me to be the person I was born to be.

> Accepting this birthright gift of self turns out to be even more demanding than attempting to become someone else. I've sometimes responded to that demand by ignoring the gift or hiding

or fleeing from it, and I don't think I'm alone. A Hasidic tale reveals both the universal tendency to want to be someone else and the importance of becoming one's self. Rabbi Zusya, when he was an old man, said, "In the coming world, they will not ask me, 'Why were you not Moses?' They will ask me, "Why were you not Zusya?'"

When we lose track of true self, how can we pick up the trail? Our lives speak through our actions and reactions, our intuitions and instincts, our feelings and bodily states, perhaps more profoundly than through words. If we can learn to read our own responses, we'll receive the guidance we need to live more authentic lives. The soul speaks only under quiet, inviting, and safe conditions. If we take some time to sit silently listening, the soul will tell us the truth about ourselves—the full, messy truth. An often-ignored dimension of the quest for wholeness is the need to embrace what we dislike about ourselves as well as what we're proud of, our liabilities as well as our strengths.

Are you in a job or life situation where you can bear the fruit that was meant to come from you? If not, what are you willing to do to make that happen? If you are doing what you do solely for money or security—no matter how nobly or spiritually—you are a hireling, a hired hand that may very well be cut off from who you are and what is important to you. If that's the case, then there is no way you will be known by the fruit you were created to bear because you aren't bearing any.

I urge you to listen in the quiet of your own heart to identify your fruit and then take steps to be in a place to bear fruit. After all, you won't ever be asked, "Why weren't you Moses or Paul?" but what will you answer if asked, "Did you bear the fruit that you were meant to produce?"

STUDY #6
WHO ARE YOU, REALLY?

It's a sad sight to see, although I encounter it every week—people who are in situations that are going nowhere, hoping that somehow their circumstances will change. Others are hoping that they themselves will change and suddenly become someone they have never been. Usually, they will quote Philippians 4:13, which states, "I can do all things through Him [Christ] who strengthens me."

Most of the time, I don't have the heart to tell them that their interpretation of Philippians 4:13 isn't correct. You *can't* be anything you want to be, nor will God change you into someone He never intended you to be in the first place. The context of Philippians 4:13 is about finances. Paul was saying he had learned to be content with a lot or a little; he had learned to be happy with what God provided at any point in time.

Anyone who is trying to be who God didn't intend for them to be is trying to do something in their own strength, not in God's strength. For example, I tried for years to be a pastor, yet no amount of trying or hiding behind Philippians 4:13 could make me a pastor. In the end, I had to face the fact that God didn't create me to be a pastor. He created me to be who I am.

So who are you? To find out, perhaps you must first admit that you are not who you are trying to be. Maybe you have taken on a role that you always desired or accepted a position that others have given you. At this point, you may have to face the reality that what you're doing isn't working, that in a sense God has withheld His favor and blessing because you are not in the right place, doing the right thing. Only then, when you've accepted who you aren't, can God show you who you are.

God wants you to know your purpose. He will not empower you to be who you are not, but He will empower you to be the fullest, greatest expression of who you are. In that setting, you will be able to do all things because God is with you. You will not be guilty of wishful thinking.

If I could personally do one thing for you right now, I would release you from trying to be who you are not. I would tell you that you haven't failed; it's just time for you to move on. Furthermore, I would look you in the eye and say, "You *can't* do all things, but you *can* do the things that God wants you to do. So stop pretending and move on. God is with you."

May you find the path where God can truly enable you to do great things for Him and other people. In other words, I hope you find the real you.

STUDY #7
BE ENCOURAGED

If I asked you what your purpose in life is, what would you say? Would you be able to give me a clear, simple set of words that describes who you are, or would you respond with a phrase that sounds nice, but doesn't really get to the heart of your existence?

While doing research for my book, *I Wrote This Book on Purpose . . . So You Can Know Yours,* I discovered author Laurence Boldt. In the introduction to his book, Boldt wrote:

> The quest for the work you love—it all begins with the two simple questions: Who am I? And What in the world am I doing here? While as old as humanity itself, these perennial questions are born anew in every man and woman who is privileged to walk upon this earth. Every sane man and woman, at some point in his or her life, is confronted by these questions—some while but children; more in adolescence and youth; still more at midlife or when facing retirement; and even the toughest customers at the death of a loved one or when they themselves have a brush with death. Yes, somewhere, sometime, we all find ourselves face to face with the questions, who am I and what am I here for.

And we do make some attempt to answer them. We ask our parents and teachers, and it seems they do not know. They refer us to political and religious institutions, which often crank out canned answers devoid of personal meaning. Some even tell us that life has no meaning, save for eating and breeding. Most of us are smart enough to recognize that canned answers or begging the question will not do. We must find real answers for ourselves. But that takes more heart and effort than we are often willing to give.[4]

Finding your purpose can be hard work, but it is well worth the effort. Your purpose not only gives you peace and a sense of destiny but also the energy and focus that will enable you to make a difference in your world. Boldt goes on to write:

Failing to find the work you love has costs, not only to your self-esteem, relationships, health, and creativity, but to your world. As a human community, we all lose when people's creative abilities do not find expression in constructive, purposeful action. We lose in terms of needless human suffering and untapped human potential. Around the globe, useless, even degrading work steals the spirit and saps the joy from the lives of millions, while much necessary work goes undone. Giving your gifts benefits the world, not only through the direct contributions you make and the joy you radiate, but through the living example you provide others of what is possible for them. Determine to play your part in creating the kind of world you want to live in.[5]

If you are still searching for your purpose, don't give up. Keep digging; keep panning; God will reward your efforts. I can't tell you when, but I promise the search will be worth it.

If you know your purpose, I want to point out one sentence from the above quote: "Around the globe, useless, even degrading work steals the spirit and saps the joy from the lives of millions, while much necessary work goes undone." Are you neglecting "necessary work" because you are giving yourself to things not related to your life purpose? If that is the case, what are you prepared to do about it?

If I can help you in your search, don't hesitate to go to www.purposequest.com, where I have posted more material to assist you. Or write me, for often I have been able to help people see what was right before them all along—their life purpose. Do what you can now to clarify and fulfill your purpose. The world is waiting for you to be clear.

STUDY #8
THAT'S ABSURD!

I always receive a lot of mail after I send my weekly email newsletter, *The Monday Memo*. Most of the time people write because they are having trouble coming to grips with discovering their specific purpose.

While I always share tips or techniques that may help you find your purpose, most often finding it comes down to hearing the voice of God. It involves recognizing that still, small voice that doesn't shout over the other voices vying for your attention. The still, small voice simply waits for you and me to stifle all the rival voices that can distract us and then quietly communicates with us.

Recently, I was reading a book by Henri Nouwen called *Making All Things New*. Nouwen wrote in it:

> From all that I said about our worried, over-filled lives, we are usually surrounded by so much inner and outer noise that it is hard to truly hear our God when he is speaking to us. We have often become deaf, unable to know when God calls us and unable to understand in which direction he calls us. Thus, our lives have become absurd. In the word absurd we find the Latin word *surdus*, which means "deaf." A spiritual life requires discipline because we need to learn to listen to God, who constantly speaks but whom we

seldom hear. When, however, we learn to listen, our lives become obedient lives. The word obedient comes from the Latin word *audire*, which means "listening." A spiritual discipline is necessary in order to move slowly from an absurd to an obedient life, from a life filled with noisy worries to a life in which there is some free inner space where we can listen to our God and follow his guidance.[6]

A life without purpose truly is an absurd life. Determine to discipline yourself to drown out or reduce the noise in your life so you can hear God. Spend some time praying and have faith that you will hear His voice. Be prepared with a pen and paper to write down what you think you hear Him say. After all, if God wants you to do His will, He will tell you what that will is. If you are to be a person of purpose, you must live an obedient life that follows the directions you hear from God. I trust and pray that you can hear Him and then obey what you hear. It really is the only way to live.

STUDY $^{\#}$9
THE WORLD IS WAITING

In a recent letter I received, someone wrote:

> Dear Doc,
>
> If only you knew what it is that you've done for me. In an age when the Internet is being used for so many horrible things...you're there.
>
> Thanks.
>
> Gideon

I include this not to draw attention to what I've done, but to encourage you to do what you are yet to do. When I started *The Monday Memo* twenty-five years ago, I had no idea how popular it would become or how God would use it to impact and direct so many lives. You never know how God will use something that you do until after you do it. You can plan and hope, dream and execute, but there is still that unexpected, unknown element that can surprise or disappoint you. The bottom line is: You must give God something to bless before He can bless it.

There was a young boy in Jesus' day who gave Jesus his lunch of five loaves of bread and two fish. Jesus took that lunch, blessed it, and distributed it to thousands. It was just a simple lunch, but in God's hands it fed a multitude with plenty left over. You need to stop focusing on how little you have in your hands and start seeing how you can get that little bit into God's hands so He can multiply it. In your hands, all you will have is stale bread and smelly fish. In God's hands, however, you may have a feast that can satisfy many others and still provide for you. The choice is yours: Hold onto what you have until it's perfect or release it now and see what happens.

You don't know what God will do with the poem you write, the song you compose, the book you write, the business you start, the class you take, or the trip you take. That's why your goals for this year are so important. If you haven't done so already, why not write down at least three specific things that you would like to accomplish in the next few months. Share these three things with someone you love and trust who can hold you accountable to get them done and will rejoice with you when they are finished. Write down not only what you will do, but also the time frame in which you will have it done. Don't try to overanalyze what to do or how to do it. Just get it out there and see how God will use it.

I believe that there are many more ideas in you, just like *The Monday Memo,* waiting to burst onto the world scene. I can't promise that you'll change the world with what you do, but I can promise that you'll change *your* world. You'll never be the same, and the joy of achievement will spur you on to even greater things. The world is waiting for what's in you; don't keep it waiting any longer.

STUDY #10
CHILDHOOD CLUES

I have visited South Africa 30 times, and I always look forward to going there. In fact, I've traveled almost 3 million miles, and I'm still excited to get on a plane and go anywhere. I had a friend who said he enjoyed taking me to the airport because he could feel my energy level rising when we were on the way there. Recently another friend asked me, "Do you still enjoy all the travel?" I replied that I do not simply enjoy it or like it, I am exhilarated by it!

My family never traveled while I was growing up, nor did we ever take a family vacation. One evening when I was about ten years old, my father took me in the car for a ride. We ended up at the Pittsburgh Airport where we spent the evening watching planes land and take off. The airport had stores, a game room, a movie theater, and an observation deck where you paid ten cents to go out on the deck and watch the planes. That was more than 50 years ago, but I can still remember the sense of excitement I had hearing the engines starting up and seeing the power of a plane during takeoff. That night, as young as I was, I vowed to go back to the airport many times when I grew up, and I have made good on my vow.

Travel is an important part of who I am and what I do. God used that childhood airport visit to put something in me that won't go away. Some childhood experiences are positive and some negative, but they all play a role in shaping who we become. Very often, there are clues to our life purpose that come early in life. Recapturing those memories can play an important role in defining your purpose.

Consider childhood stories of the following people:

As a child in England, he spent hours creating cardboard sets for his puppet shows to entertain his family. – Andrew Lloyd Webber, producer of the theatrical rendition of *Phantom of the Opera*

Cut from his basketball team as a youngster, he still dreamed of playing basketball one day. – Michael Jordan, the world's greatest player

Swimming to gain strength in his two broken arms, this teenager changed dreams from becoming an astronaut to aquanaut. – Jacques Cousteau, famous underwater explorer

This young boy was fascinated with anatomical diagrams in the *World Book Encyclopedia*. – Jonas Salk, who developed the polio vaccine

This college dropout had ideas about information access. – Bill Gates, founder of Microsoft and at one time the world's richest man

What was your favorite game as a child? What did you spend time daydreaming about? What did you do as a child that made you the happiest? What positive or negative experiences led you to make a life-shaping decision that is still with you today? Have you lost contact with some part of your youth that could once again provide you with purpose and excitement?

As you search your past, you may find keys to the present that will unlock your future. Why not spend some time thinking about your childhood with a writing tablet in front of you? Write down what you remember and see if there are any childhood clues that emerge to help you define your purpose. You may have an experience like my airport visit that can reshape your adult life if you let it.

STUDY #11
FILLED WITH THE SPIRIT

I was thinking about a man in the Bible named Bezalel. It is said about this man that he was "filled with the Spirit of God." Now, I don't know about you, but when I see or hear that phrase, I assume that the person who is "filled" is probably a holy man, preacher, or saint. Surely, he was "filled with the Spirit" to perform miracles, preach, or fulfill some other religious activity. With Bezalel, however, this was not the case.

> Then the Lord said to Moses, "See, I have chosen Bezalel son of Uri, the son of Hur, of the tribe of Judah, and I have filled him with the Spirit of God, with skill, ability and knowledge in all kinds of crafts-to make artistic designs for work in gold, silver and bronze, to cut and set stones, to work in wood, and to engage in all kinds of craftsmanship" (Exodus 31:1-5).

Bezalel wasn't full of the Spirit to do religious things; he was full of the Spirit to work with his hands and create artistic masterpieces. He was an exceptional craftsman, which was the will of God for Bezalel's life. God gave him special ability and gave him His "Spirit" to excel in some area of creativity.

When searching for our God-given purpose, too

often we limit the search to activities normally associated with church work. We may not think that the "Spirit" may be on us to write, teach a class, paint, sing opera, run a business, or lead a government agency. The passage above lets us know that life purpose isn't restricted to church work. Your purpose may take you to places you didn't previously consider to be part of God's purpose for you.

Do you like to work with your hands? Can you fix or create things? Do you have an eye for beauty, color, or symmetry? Then why can't some expression of those things be your life purpose? You don't have to preach or counsel to do God's will. You can create beautiful things that bring pleasure to God and others and be in the center of God's will for your life.

What are you "filled with the Spirit" to do? Don't see that as a hobby, and don't wait until you can do something more "spiritual" before you feel you're doing the will of God. It's time for the painters to paint, the poets to rhyme, the singers to sing, the writers to write, the conductors to conduct, and the dancers to dance. If we can find people who are "filled with the Spirit" to do those things, the world will be a better place and God's will shall be done.

STUDY #12
THE MUSIC OF THE FUTURE

Occasionally, I run into a quote and desperately wish I had said it myself because it's so powerful. I heard one of those quotes one morning in church, looked at my wife, and said, "I've got to write about that!" To the best of my research, this quote can be attributed to "Captain" Bob Smith, a motivational speaker and it goes like this: "Hope is hearing the music of the future. Faith is dancing to it today!"

Both clarifying your purpose and setting goals involve hearing the music of the future. You look beyond where you are and what you're doing to see yourself from God's perspective. You see yourself doing what you were born to do and achieving what you are here to achieve, even though you're not at that place yet. As you read this study, aren't you really listening for a certain sound that provides clarity and direction? When you hear it, you will begin to tap your foot, and before you know it, you will be dancing to a tune that no one else can hear.

Once you see your purpose or visualize a goal, you need to have faith to walk it out in everyday life. In other words, you should begin to dance to the music of the future by preparing yourself in faith to be the greatest expression of your purpose that you can be. You can take intermediate steps today that will help you reach your goal tomorrow.

Please open your ears and heart to hear your life

music. It may be a faint sound or only one musical phrase, but it's playing. Have hope that God will let you hear some of that music now. Then, when you hear the music, have faith! Take some steps that will prepare you to achieve your destiny and fulfill your life purpose.

"Hope is hearing the music of the future. Faith is dancing to it today!" I trust you will hear the music of the future and not just the monotonous sounds of the past and present. I hope you will catch a glimpse of what you can be and not just see what you've been. If you've been dancing with your present self, I encourage you to change partners and dance with the you of the future. You need to get acquainted, this present and future you, and as a team, you will both do great things.

STUDY #13
ARE YOU HAPPY?

Are you happy? I didn't ask if you were reasonably satisfied. I asked if you are happy. I'm not sure you can say you're happy just because you aren't sad. Do you have enthusiasm for what you do? Is there a joy in your heart and life that energizes you? If not, what price are you willing to pay to get in touch with that level of happiness?

Several years ago, I asked myself that question, and the answer was no. One day, I found myself sitting on a plane and began a conversation with the man next to me. He was going to a convention to make a speech, which is what he did for a living. He had written a book entitled, *If Aristotle Ran General Motors*, and made a good living talking about his book to businesspeople. As he was sharing with me what he did, I said to myself, "That's what I want to do!" I didn't want to talk about Aristotle to businesspeople, but I did want to travel and speak about my passion in front of anyone who would listen. I wasn't happy doing what I was doing then—it was time to do something else.

Joy is a barometer, an indicator that tells you if you are on course in your life and career. If you're doing what you do and have money as your main or perhaps only motivation, then you are a "hireling," renting out your skills to the highest bidder. If you have the money but not the joy, you are missing the main fuel for creativity, meaning, and fulfillment. If your joy is gone and you're unhappy, that may be reason enough to begin considering your options. Do you want to spend the rest of your life feeling like you do now?

I am not suggesting we worship at the altar of happiness as a life purpose. Joy is an important indication you are functioning in your purpose, but that doesn't mean you won't have troubles and challenges. The joy is there to carry you through those tough times. Nehemiah said it when he exhorted the people, "The joy of the Lord is your strength" (Nehemiah 8:10). If you aren't happy, you may not have the strength you need to fulfill your purpose. In fact, if you aren't happy, you may not be in your purpose at all.

I was asked at a church seminar one time, "Dr. Stanko, where is the cross in what you teach?" The woman had a legitimate question. Was I promoting a selfish pursuit of personal pleasure and hiding it behind what I called "doing the will of God" in fulfilling our purpose? I answered by referring to the Apostle Paul, a man of purpose.

Paul's purpose was to preach the gospel to the Gentiles, which is where he had his greatest success. There was plenty of "cross" in Paul's purpose. Just read Second Corinthians, chapters four and eleven, to see what hardship he endured and pressure he was under. Yet the joy of his purpose carried him through all those things, and later he wrote, "I have fought the good fight, I have finished the race, I have kept the faith" (2 Timothy 4:7). His joy empowered him to finish.

Regarding my own purpose, I love creating order out of chaos but, if the truth be known, doing it in church settings isn't always my favorite work. Yet it's the will of God for me. When I bring order, I feel His joy and presence, but the cross is present as well. Jesus, for the joy set before Him, endured His cross and despised His shame (see Hebrews 12:1-2). He couldn't deny or refuse His joy; for anyone to do so would make the trials of life an almost intolerable burden.

What about you? Are you cut off from your joy? Are you happy? Meditate on these questions and see what answers you come up with. I hope you will answer honestly and set your heart to do whatever it takes to reconnect your life with your joy.

STUDY #14
WHAT OPTIONS DO YOU HAVE?

I receive a lot of feedback from people who are "stuck" in jobs that aren't related to their life purpose. "What do we do with our years of seniority and assurance of a decent salary, when we don't feel connected to our purpose?" Let me answer this question by making a few points:

1. *Know your purpose.* Most people who can't see how to get out of their current job usually don't have a clear, concise purpose statement. It's hard to see how you can move on until you have a vision of where you're going. Recently, I was talking with a woman who was working for a bank, although she loved to improve women's self-esteem through all kinds of practical training. She also enjoyed doing hair, nails, and other beauty-related activities. Our entire conversation focused on what her life purpose was. Because she went away clear about her purpose when we ended our conversation, she had ideas of what she could do after her bank job (where she was encountering many problems).

2. *Choose wisely.* It is important that you choose jobs that are best suited for you and your talents whenever possible. Stephen Covey warns not to start climbing a ladder until you're sure it's leaning against the right wall! If

possible, don't take a job simply because it's offered to you. Ask yourself whether the job or career has the potential to release you to growth and joy. If it doesn't, then don't take it. If you do, you may be writing me in five years asking how you can get out! That is tough to do, for the financial obligations at that point may necessitate that you stay put, even though you're not content.

3. *Work hard.* I know that you already work hard, but when you know your purpose, your real work may begin at 5:00 p.m. when you end your day job and are finally free to embrace your purpose. For years, I wrote, taught, and studied after my regular workday was over. I spent time preparing for the day when I would be released to speak and consult. I developed expertise on my jobs that would add to the repertoire of services I could eventually offer. The woman I mentioned above is probably going to have to go to night school to get the certification she needs to fulfill her purpose. Many times, there is no way around making that sacrifice.

It occurred to me this past week that Jesus was a carpenter and Paul made tents, but neither man ever talked about their trade. In both cases, someone else told us about their occupations. Certainly Paul never mentioned what he did for a living. Yet in every letter he wrote, Paul talked about his purpose of bringing the gospel to the Gentiles. He talked about his life, not in terms of what he did to make money, but in terms of what he did to change the world. You must begin to define yourself not in terms of what you are doing but in terms of who you are at the core of your being. That's where your purpose resides.

If you are "stuck," first tell me what your purpose is. From there, what steps can you take to fulfill it, even if it is only part-time or on weekends? It may not be much, but for now it's the best option. Don't wait until next week to do something about this situation; do it now. It is said that every journey starts with the first step. Take your first step now by reading a book, enrolling for a class, setting aside two nights for your second business, or beginning to research a new career in earnest. Start making your way out of your dead-end road and see if you can't find the highway of purpose.

STUDY #15
THE PIECES OF YOUR PAST

I try to read a book every month that focuses on the topics of purpose and productivity. One such book I recently read was *Forgetting Ourselves on Purpose* by Brian Mahan. In the book, Mahan describes a childhood experience of Dorothy Day, founder of the Catholic Worker Movement on the Lower East Side of New York City. As I have mentioned in the past, childhood dreams, failures, and goals can hold clues to help you find your purpose. Mahan quotes Day's own words:

> I think my "pilgrimage" began when I was a child, when I was seven or eight . . . I'm sitting with my mother, and she's telling me about some trouble in the world, about children like me who don't have enough food—they're dying. I'm eating a doughnut, I think. I ask my mother why other children don't have doughnuts and I do . . . . I don't remember her words, but I can still see her face; it's the face of someone who is sad, and resigned. . . Most of all, I remember trying to understand what it meant—me eating a doughnut, and lots of children with no food at all. . . . I don't remember my words, I just remember holding the doughnut up and hoping she'd take it and give it to someone, some child . . . . I didn't

eat that doughnut! I put it down on the kitchen table. . . . I asked her if God knew someone nearby, or if He could help us with our modest doughnut plan. . . . I don't remember asking her that, asking her how we might enlist God in this effort; but she says I kept talking about God and Jesus and feeding the hungry with doughnuts, until she told me, please, to stop![7]

Here was an adult woman immersed in something significant for the poor and the signs of her purpose first became clear in a childhood conversation with her mother. It's interesting that Day's mother told her to stop talking about her "doughnut plan." All too often, we stop talking about our passion because it doesn't make sense, or we don't see how we can possibly do it as an adult and yet make a living. To her credit, Day may have stopped talking about her plan, but she never stopped thinking about it. She took some social action to correct a problem in the best way she knew how.

My life purpose is to create order out of chaos. In my own life, I remember my favorite rainy-day activity was to disorganize my room so I could put it back in order! I remember "attacking" my father's messy garage as an eight-year-old to put it in order. When I did, I stood there and beheld my work with a strange sense of peace.

If your parents are still alive, maybe it's time to talk with them. If not, are there brothers, sisters, aunts, uncles, or close family friends you can talk to? Ask them what you were like and what they remember about you when you were a child. What did you talk about? What games did you play? Something may stand out to them that will provide you a clue as to your purpose.

I can't tell you when you will find your purpose. That varies from person to person. My objective is to help you identify it when it does come to you, so you won't dismiss it as insignificant or irrelevant information. Why not investigate your past and see what purpose clues emerge? Write down everything you know already, plus any childhood clues you obtain from your family, and study your notes. Do you see any pattern? Don't panic if you don't, but keep adding to that page, so that one day you will look at it and realize you have all the pieces of the purpose puzzle, and the picture is clear.

STUDY #16
WE CAN'T DO IT UNTIL WE KNOW IT

It seems that there's no end to the interest generated by the purpose message. Every week, I meet with many people individually and in groups to help them find their purpose. *The Monday Memo* regularly has purpose as its theme and focus, and I receive many inquiries and questions online throughout the week. I have found one recurring problem among those who aren't sure yet as to what their purpose is—trying to understand how they will fulfill it before they even know what it is.

I talk to wives who are concerned about how their purpose will affect their families, but when I ask them what their purpose is, they can't tell me. I talk to husbands who ask questions about finances, career changes, and time away from home. When I ask them what their purpose is, they often respond, "Well, it's sort of like, well, you know, to maybe encourage people and to, uh, glorify God. Yeah, that's it!" That's probably not it.

Until you have a clear statement of your purpose, everything after remains unclear. There's no way you can understand how your purpose will work itself out until you know what it is. Therefore, your primary job is not to figure out the outcome, but to have faith to find your purpose in the first place. When you do, the rest seems to fall in place, sometimes quickly, sometimes over a longer period.

It's critical that you make a clear sound when describing your purpose. The Apostle Paul wrote the following analogy in one of his letters:

> Even in the case of lifeless things that make sounds, such as the flute or harp, how will anyone know what tune is being played unless there is a distinction in the notes? Again, if the trumpet does not sound a clear call, who will get ready for battle? (1 Corinthians 14:7-8).

Once you find your purpose and can clearly describe it in nonreligious terms, you will recognize the opportunities that come your way. Whether you're finding or fulfilling your purpose, there's one key element to your success, and that's faith. You can't "figure out" your purpose, nor can you then set out to accomplish it in the power of your own effort.

I've found it takes more faith to find your purpose than it does to fulfill it! That's why it's so critical you are clear on what it is. Once you see it, faith will rise in you to see it done. Your purpose is what Paul referred to as "the vision from heaven" (Acts 26:19). That can only come when heaven is ready to release it, and you are ready to receive it.

It took a lot more time and effort to realize what my purpose was than to find its expression. Are you ready to find your purpose? I can't promise that you will find it this week, but I can urge you to have faith that you will find it, if not this week, then in the weeks to come. You will seek, work, and strive to define your purpose, but in all of that, you must trust that God will show it to you. When you see it, you will be like the parable found in Matthew 13:44:

> "The kingdom of heaven is like treasure hidden in a field. When a man found it, he hid it again, and then in his joy went and sold all he had and bought that field."

I hope God helps clarify your purpose. If it happens, you won't have problems knowing what to do. You'll go for it because you'll have found the treasure worth the pursuit.

STUDY #17
WHY ARE YOU DOING IT?

I had a meeting with someone who had a job offer. It was a good job that she had done before and could undoubtedly do again with a high level of excellence and efficiency. There was only one problem: She didn't want to do it! There were others who hoped that she would want to do it. She valued their input and searched her heart to find some way to fulfill their expectations. She had to say "no" to their offer, however, and instead launched out on her own to find something better suited to her life purpose.

Defining yourself and setting a course that you feel good about are difficult things to do. It's often easier to follow the career path of least resistance, a path that often can provide job security. For years, I felt I was supposed to be a pastor. I tried to live up to those expectations that, to be honest, I put on myself. I thought that's what God wanted me to do. I was a pastor to please others, but I wasn't happy. Finally, I faced how unhappy I was and resigned. Since then, I've resisted attempts by friends and counselors to fashion me according to what they felt I should do. Instead, I set out on a path to define and fulfill my purpose.

Now you may be asking, "What about the will of God? Where does that come into play?" And those are good questions. My sense, however, is that God will give you the will and heart to do His work. There may be a season where you do something that crosses your will and separates you from your joy, but I don't think that can happen for very long.

There's a Bible verse from *The Living Bible* that reads: "For God is at work within you, helping you want to obey him, and then helping you do what he wants" (Philippians 2:13). God is working in you to give you a will and desire to fulfill His will and then helping you do what that will represents. Part of that help is His joy. A man named Nehemiah once said, "The joy of the Lord is your strength" (Nehemiah 8:10). If you have no joy in what you do, then you have no strength.

Why are you doing what you do? Why are you studying what you are studying? Why are you running the business that you are running? Is it to fulfill someone else's dreams and expectations? If so, is that a good enough reason to continue doing it? The answer may be "yes," but it also may be "no." That's something only you can answer. If you answer "no," then what are you prepared to do about it?

It may be time to be honest with yourself and face the fact that you can't live up to others' expectations. You must live your own life and fulfill your own purpose. If you do nothing else but face this reality, you will have taken a giant step to finding and fulfilling your purpose. May you find a breakthrough soon as you find the courage to define yourself. There's no one better suited for the job.

STUDY #18
FREE TO BE ME

I ran across another great quote as I was thinking about how hard it is to simply be yourself. Parents, family, educators, and friends may have told you that you can't do this or that because you won't be able to make a living, or because it just doesn't make sense to them. At other times, you may have been your own worst enemy, criticizing and putting down your own creativity and tendencies. I talk with many people who are spending more time and energy trying to be who they are not, instead of becoming the best expression of who God created them to be. I can't find who said this, so if you know, please pass the name on to me:

Work like you don't need the money.

Love like you've never been hurt.

Dance like nobody's watching.

Sing like nobody's listening.

Read that over a few times and let the words and message sink in. Those lines speak of freedom—freedom to be who God made you to be without concern for what others think. It also speaks of having freedom from past hurts, disappointments, and failures so that you can pursue the unique path that is yours. Finally, those lines set you free from yourself and your tendency to prematurely judge what you are becoming or doing.

There's a proverb that states, "The fear of man brings a snare" (Proverbs 29:25). If you can't be who you were created to be because you're afraid of what someone thinks, you have indeed fallen into a trap. Instead of responding to your inner voice, you are following outside voices that don't understand you or the path God has chosen for you. You need to give yourself permission to sing and dance like no one else is paying attention.

Why not spend some time discovering where you have limited your development because of what others think. Write down any areas or interests that you had a desire to pursue at one time only to have someone talk you out of them. Maybe you have talked yourself out of them. Whoever is to blame, determine to reestablish contact with the song and dance that are uniquely yours. As you do, I hope you'll take some steps, no matter how small, toward freedom of the mind and heart, freedom toward the fulfillment that comes from being true to the real you. I'm free to be me. I recommend it to you as a worthy goal.

STUDY #19
PERMISSION TO BE CREATIVE

When I travel, I bring several books to read and study. On one trip, I brought *The Artist's Way* by Julia Cameron. The subtitle of this book is "A Spiritual Path to Higher Creativity," and it's a best seller, available in its tenth anniversary edition. The stated purpose of the book is to provide a course in discovering and recovering your creative self. I would recommend the book as a tool to develop the disciplines necessary for creativity.

There are many helpful tips throughout the book to help you unlock and release your creativity, such as:

- Stop telling yourself, "It's too late."
- Stop waiting until you make enough money to do something you'd really love.
- Stop telling yourself, "It's just my ego" whenever you yearn for a more creative life.
- Stop telling yourself that your dreams don't matter, that they are only dreams and that you should be more sensible.
- Stop fearing that your family and friends would think you crazy.
- Stop telling yourself that creativity is a luxury and that you should be grateful for what you've got.[8]

The author continues:

> As you learn to recognize, nurture, and protect
> your inner artist, you will be able to move be-
> yond pain and creative constriction. You will
> learn ways to recognize and resolve fear, remove
> emotional scar tissue, and strengthen your con-
> fidence. Damaging old ideas about creativity will
> be explored and discarded.[8]

Do any of these statements apply to you? Maybe it's
time you examined your own attitude toward creativity. Is
your definition of creativity restricted to artists and writers? Maybe your creativity lies in other areas. Do you like
to work with wood or metal? Are you a sculptor or someone who likes to work with ceramics? Or perhaps you are
a seamstress, a cook, or a baker? Then again, you may have
a house you've always wanted to design and build, or an
idea for a business. Whatever your expression of creativity,
what are you prepared to do about it? If nothing else, you
may have to confront your low self-esteem concerning your
creativity by going to the kitchen or workshop and getting
your hands dirty.

This issue is critical if you are going to live a purposeful and productive life. You must learn to trust that
which is within you, that which has come from God who is
the source of all that is creative. I've gotten into the habit of
studying creative people who were writers, actors, compos-
ers, or poets. I want to study those masters so I can become
a master in my own right. Will you join me and explore and
develop your creative side? I hope you will and that you'll
give yourself permission to be creative.

STUDY #20
THE JONAH COMPLEX

The famous psychologist, Dr. Abraham Maslow, coined a term "The Jonah Complex." What did Maslow mean? We know that Jonah was an Old Testament prophet and that he had a short book that related part of his life story. Jonah was given an assignment by God to go and deliver a harsh message to a city and a people he didn't like. He didn't want to do it, so he got on a ship and went in the opposite direction from where he was told to go.

A storm arose during the trip, and it soon became clear to the sailors that Jonah was the cause of the storm. When they threw him overboard, the storm ceased, and Jonah was swallowed by a whale; Jonah then spent three days and nights in the whale's stomach. After Jonah relented and agreed to go on God's mission, the whale spit him out and Jonah went on his way.

Maslow used "The Jonah Complex" to describe anyone who is running from their true life's calling. He went on to say, "If you deliberately set out to be less than you are capable of, you will never truly be happy." [9] This term accurately describes the condition of many people with whom I have come in contact. They are running from the greatness and creativity that is in them. They are afraid, not of failure, but of success.

So what do these people do who are trapped in "The

Jonah Complex"? According to my experience, they spend a lot of time trying to weather the storm. They try to stay on the ship where they are, instead of jumping into the waves of life. They tell me they are "praying about it"—whatever the "it" is for them. Yet day after day, and sometimes year after year, goes by and they do nothing. Their prayer is a delay tactic, waiting for God to do something that only they can do.

What about you? Are you suffering from "The Jonah Complex"? Are you running from your purpose or from some significant thing that God has for you to do? Is your ship being tossed by the waves of financial lack, unhappiness, and lack of productivity, yet you stubbornly cling to the ship's mast, hoping that things will get better? I've found that many know their purpose but are afraid for whatever reason to walk it out. Perhaps it's time for you to face who you are and what God wants you to do. And perhaps it's time for you to take steps to get off your sinking ship and into the purpose of God. It may look more dangerous "out there," but the only danger lies in avoiding the great things that God has for you to do.

STUDY #21
YES AND NO

I usually begin purpose seminars with Acts 6:1-4:

In those days when the number of disciples was increasing, the Grecian Jews among them complained against the Hebraic Jews because their widows were being overlooked in the daily distribution of food. So the Twelve gathered all the disciples together and said, "It would not be right for us to neglect the ministry of the word of God to wait on tables. Brothers, choose seven men from among you who are known to be full of the Spirit and wisdom. We will turn this responsibility over to them and will give our attention to prayer and the ministry of the word."

I study this passage regularly, and it speaks to me every time I do. Three things impress me most:

- There were problems, even in the early church.
- The apostles could not solve or be involved in all the problems.
- The apostles focused on what they did best.

I like this passage so much because it portrays a problem you and I have all the time: when to say "yes" and when to say "no." The more successful you are, the more this problem seems to appear because success only leads to more opportunities and "open doors." I talk with people regularly who are facing those "open doors," but for whatever reason find themselves unable to walk through them.

Sometimes the problem is what you are currently doing. It's familiar; you have had a measure of success or at least know what's expected of you. The current situation may provide a safe environment in which to function. If you continue doing what you currently do, you won't be able to embrace that new thing, opportunity, or "open door" that's before you.

At other times, you may have an "open door," but as you begin to walk through, a new development in your current situation comes to confuse and distract you. It may be more money, a slight variation in your current routine, or an offer of some new responsibility that causes you to reconsider that "open door." The Apostle Paul wrote, "Because a great door for effective work has opened to me, and there are many who oppose me" (1 Corinthians 16:9). Sometimes the opposition presents itself as a chance to stay in your comfort zone where you know the people and the routine.

I ran across a quote this week that may help. It is from Baruch Spinoza, a 17th century Dutch philosopher. He wrote, "A good thing which prevents us from enjoying a greater good is in truth an evil." I'm sure the apostles in Acts 6 saw helping the widows as a good thing but helping them would have taken them away from something better. Thus, they declined to get personally involved.

Ask yourself if some good thing is keeping you from a better thing and has thus become a bad thing for you. If the answer is "yes," then what are you prepared to do about it? Do you have the courage and faith to face that good thing and stop doing it? Are you prepared to say "no" to find your greater "yes"? Don't settle for good when you can have the best. You owe it to God, yourself, and others not to do that.

STUDY #22

A LETTER FROM JACQUIE

I received an email one time that perfectly portrayed what I want for your life. Let me share it with you:

Dear Mr. Stanko,

I felt a need to write and thank you for the beautiful *Monday Memos*. They have altered the course of my life, and I just want to share the wonderful miracles that have happened to me.

I was feeling that my life had no purpose, and I was lost. I came across *The Monday Memo* and things began to change. I found direction and my purpose was made clear to me in my prayers. For years I have wanted to go to America to learn how to help autistic children. You see, I have an autistic son, but such a trip has never worked out. After 5 years I thought I would try again. Well, to cut a long story short, I am going to finally make the trip and learn how to help my son! When I get back to Zimbabwe, I am going to start a school here that will help other autistic and mentally challenged children. Since I have found my purpose and my dream, I feel alive. I am bubbling inside and feel like I am bouncing off the ceiling and walls.

It is a miracle. I am a single parent with three children and not finding it easy living in this environment where everything goes up daily. The thought of a trip to America seemed impossible.

I had faith and believed that if it was meant to be, it would happen. I was given the money for my ticket, and I was also given a huge scholarship for the education and accommodation in America. I also received a visa, which is another impossible task in this country. God has smoothed my road and is helping me to achieve my dream. I am just so very happy and grateful. I leave soon and feel so very, very blessed.

I want to thank you from the bottom of my heart for helping me on my way by making me think differently. God bless you and the wonderful work that you do. – Jacquie

No, Jacquie, I must thank you. Thank you for having the faith to pursue both your purpose and the means to achieve it. Thank you too for turning a difficult situation into one that will bless not only your family but so many others. On behalf of purpose seekers everywhere, thank you for giving us a powerful example of faith and purpose.

When I read Jacquie's letter, I thought of an anonymous poem that I found years ago:

There's no thrill in easy sailing
  when the skies are clear and blue.
There's no joy in merely doing things
  that anyone can do.
But there is some satisfaction
  that is mighty sweet to take.
When you reach a destination
  that you thought you'd never make.

Wherever you are in your purpose journey, I hope that you are closer to your destination. If you are discouraged with the journey, don't give up. You may be closer than you think to writing someone a letter like Jacquie wrote me. Happy trails!

STUDY #23
WHAT DO YOU FEAR?

I purchased a new laptop computer a couple years ago. I put off getting it, even though many of the keys and features on my old one didn't function any longer. Why did I hesitate? It wasn't only because of the cost; it was also because I was afraid of the change from the old one to the new.

What was I afraid of? I was afraid my technical ignorance would show. I was also afraid of losing data in the transfer, or of being on the road somewhere and the new unit would fail to operate. I was even afraid of choosing the wrong unit to replace the old one. Those fears kept me from deciding. After I made the purchase, I was relieved, although I spent more than a few hours working to get the new computer just the way I desired it to be.

You may want to ask yourself, "What am I afraid of?" In my discussions with many people, I have found three basic fears that can keep people from being purposeful and productive. They are:

- Fear of others
- Fear of failure
- Fear of looking foolish

Let's address the first one on the list. A wise writer once wrote: "Fear of man will prove to be a snare, but whoever trusts in the Lord is kept safe" (Proverbs 29:25).

I get many emails from people who are afraid of their supervisor, pastor, spouse or counselor. This fear keeps them bound to the past so they can't respond in faith to the future. They can't embrace change, not because they fear the change but because they fear people's reaction to their change.

The second fear is of failure. I know how painful failures can be because I've had my share of them. But failures have been great teachers, and every failure has produced enough wisdom to prepare me for future success. I'm reminded of that well-known Bible verse that states: "And we know that in all things God works for the good of those who love him, who have been called according to his purpose" (Romans 8:28).

God is working in all things for you. Don't go looking for failure and don't do stupid things expecting God to cover you. If you are facing a decision that lines up with your purpose and God's will for your life, then take the next step toward achieving that purpose, without fear of failure. If you should fail, learn from it and move on.

Finally, if you're afraid of looking foolish, then perhaps you had better go live in a desert where no one can see you. Learning and growing can make you look awkward. Think of it like a child learning to walk. They look foolish as they take a few steps and fall, yet they persevere with the encouragement of their family. They overcome their foolishness only to enter the next learning experience that has the potential to make them look just as foolish. Jesus said:

> "Do not be afraid, little flock, for your Father has been pleased to give you the kingdom. Sell your possessions and give to the poor. Provide purses for yourselves that will not wear out, a treasure in heaven that will not be exhausted, where no thief comes near, and no moth destroys. For

where your treasure is, there your heart will be also" (Luke 12:32-34).

Determine not to yield to fear any longer! It wasn't until I began to face my fears that I was able to overcome them. Today I still deal with fear, but I no longer let it be my master. I now ask myself, "John, what are you afraid of?" and then I proceed. I would urge you to do the same.

STUDY #24
WHAT YOU DO
ISN'T WHO YOU ARE

I read and enjoyed a book by Os Guinness, entitled *Entrepreneurs of Life: Faith and the Venture of Purposeful Living.* As I read, I began to reflect on the difference between one's occupation and one's purpose. As the word implies, an occupation is what uses up our time and energy. Your occupation is what pays the bills, but it isn't necessarily what defines who you are. To further explain, let's look at the Apostle Paul's life.

Paul's purpose was to bring the gospel of Christ to the Gentile world. We know that because his "call" on the Damascus road has a prominent place in the book of Acts. In every epistle that Paul wrote, he made some reference to his purpose, usually relating his purpose to some Old Testament passage. When Paul talked about himself, he referred to his purpose, yet that purpose wasn't his occupation.

To earn a living, Paul made tents. When he moved into an area and lacked funds, he went to work as a tent maker. Yet Paul never talked or wrote about his occupation. The only way we know that Paul made tents was that Luke wrote about it in the book of Acts. Don't you find it interesting that Paul never referred to it? That was what he did, but it wasn't who he was. He was an apostle to the Gentiles and that is what got the choice place in his heart, time, efforts, and writings.

Who are you? I'm not asking what you do. You may sell insurance, but who are you? You may also be a missionary to some people group, while selling insurance pays the bills. When people ask you what you do, like I just did, how do you respond? Do you say that you're an insurance salesperson or a missionary? If you answer that you're a salesperson, then you're defining yourself according to what you do. If you say missionary, you're focusing on purpose and not on what provides your food and pays the bills. You may only get to the mission field once a year on your vacation time, but the other weeks you're praying and working toward that mission. You don't have to quit your occupation to embrace your purpose. You may simply need to distinguish between the two.

Guinness wrote, in the book I mentioned above, the following paragraph (since he uses the words "calling" and "vocation" for purpose, I have taken the liberty of inserting the word "purpose" where appropriate):

> Calling [purpose] helps us finish [our lives] well because it prevents us from confusing the termination of our occupations with the termination of our vocations [purpose]. If we ever limit our calling [purpose] to what we do, and that task is taken away from us—we suddenly find ourselves unemployed, retired, or pronounced terminally ill—then we are tempted to depression and doubt. What has happened? We have let our occupation become so intertwined with our vocation [purpose] that losing the occupation means losing the sense of vocation [purpose] too.[10]

Have you either not found or lost your sense of purpose? Perhaps you have confused the difference between what you do and who you are. I would suggest you take time to reflect on this important distinction. No longer be content to define your life in terms of what you do but rather who you are. It will make all the difference in the world.

STUDY #25
DEALING WITH DISCOURAGEMENT

If you are discouraged while trying to find your purpose, I understand how you feel. It can be hard work! I can
guarantee that you'll find your purpose, but I can't tell you
when that will happen! The search can be long and frus-
trating. I heard a principle shared once by someone who
was looking for their place in God's plan. This person began
to thank God for his purpose before he knew what it was.
Now that's faith!

Thanking God for what you already have before you
see or know it is consistent with faith, for Paul wrote: "As
it is written: 'I have made you [Abraham] a father of many
nations.' He is our father in the sight of God, in whom he
believed—the God who gives life to the dead and calls
things that are not as though they were" (Romans 4:17).
God seems to talk about things that are not as though they
are. Why don't you do the same? Talk about and thank God
for your purpose as if you already know it. It's just a matter
of time before you do.

If you know your purpose, but are discouraged in
fulfilling it, why not try something new? I want you to close
your eyes and picture yourself doing what you were created to do. See yourself conducting an orchestra, singing a

song, working with wood, or running your business. When I'm writing a book and I get discouraged with its progress, I close my eyes and picture myself signing that book and handing it to someone. Before I have it finished, I choose to "see" it finished and being given to someone else (who is always smiling when they receive it). For some strange reason, that image always encourages me to keep writing. When I do this, I feel like I'm borrowing some joy from tomorrow to take pleasure in today.

Finally, if you know your purpose but for some reason find yourself in a down time, do what I did recently. The phone wasn't ringing, I had some cancellations, and money was a bit scarce. So I began to read the emails and letters I received over the last year. I chose to focus on what God has already done, believing that He would open doors for me to do it again.

When there's no one around to encourage you, then you sometimes must encourage yourself. Remember the lives you've touched, the songs you've written, or the other success stories of which you've been part. If you don't already, begin to save up mementos of your successes so you can refer to them in your down times.

Finally, sometimes you need a friend who can perk you up when you're down. Don't be too proud or afraid to call them. Sometimes other people can see your purpose and productivity more clearly than you. Still others can point out your potential while you are still in the development stage. Listen to what they have to say! And if I can be of assistance, please don't hesitate to write me. I'm familiar with many of the pitfalls on the road of purpose and will be glad to encourage you along the way as you battle your discouragement.

STUDY #26
FOR GOD, IN GOD

Once while teaching in Zimbabwe, I talked about the difference between doing things *in God* and doing things *for God*. When you are working in God, you are working with the strength and energy that God provides. When you are working for God, you usually work in your own strength and the results are seldom what you want. When Moses was working for God, he killed an Egyptian. Later, when he worked in God, he raised his staff, and the entire Egyptian army was destroyed. That's the difference between "in-God" and "for-God" results. When you find and work in your life purpose, you almost always produce "in-God" results; that's why knowing your purpose is so important.

I was recently reading about John Wesley, the founder of the Methodist church. John Wesley found his purpose and therefore was able to produce "in-God" results. Read on and see what I mean: Wesley would preach three times a day, beginning at 5:00 a.m. since workers could stop to hear him as they walked to their daily drudgery. He sometimes covered 60 miles a day on horseback. Weather conditions made no difference; he made his schedule and kept it regardless. He would flee an angry mob by jumping into a cold pond, swim out, and go on to preach again. He had the ability to turn hostile people his way. In all he went to Ireland 42 times and to Scotland 22 times.

John Wesley taught as much by example as by his measured sermons. He published many volumes for use in devotions and turned profits into such projects as a dispensary for the poor. His personal life was beyond reproach. He translated hymns, interpreted scripture, wrote hundreds of letters, trained hundreds of men and women, and kept in his journals a record of expended energy that has hardly a rival in western literature.

He made this diary entry on Tuesday, June 28, 1774:

> This being my birthday, the first day of my seventy-second year, I was considering: How is this, that I find just the same strength as I did thirty years ago? That my sight is considerably better now, and my nerves firmer than they were then? That I have none of the infirmities of old age, and have lost several I had in my youth? The grand reason is the good pleasure of God, who doth whatsoever pleaseth him. The chief means are: 1) my constantly rising at four, for about fifty years; 2) my generally preaching at five in the morning, one of the most healthy exercises in the world; 3) my never travelling less, by sea or land, than four thousand five hundred miles a year.

During his ministry, Wesley rode over 250,000 miles on horseback, a distance equal to ten circuits of the globe along the equator. He preached over 40,000 sermons. Today his followers number 40 million people.[11]

Ask yourself whether you are achieving "in-God" or "for-God" results. Are you accomplishing all that you were created to do, or are you achieving far below your potential? If you aren't happy with your results, then maybe you need to meditate on the difference between working in God or for God. I trust that you will find a way to work in God and that you will change the world, just as John Wesley did.

STUDY #27
WHAT MAKES YOU CRY?

There's a man in the Bible named Nehemiah who was the cupbearer for the king. In other words, he was a butler or a servant. We aren't told how he came to this trusted position, and we don't know much about Nehemiah's background. He just shows up on the scene as a servant. Service to others is how many of God's leaders were prepared for leadership: If you are a servant leader, someone may take your leadership away, but they can never take away your ability or desire to serve. That's the constant factor in every servant leader's life.

That isn't what I want to show you from the life of Nehemiah. While he was serving, a group of people came to visit from Jerusalem:

> The words of Nehemiah son of Hacaliah: In the month of Kislev in the twentieth year, while I was in the citadel of Susa, Hanani, one of my brothers, came from Judah with some other men, and I questioned them about the Jewish remnant that survived the exile, and also about Jerusalem. They said to me, "Those who survived the exile and are back in the province are in great trouble and disgrace. The wall of Jerusalem is broken down, and its gates have been burned with fire" (Nehemiah 1:1-3).

First, Nehemiah questioned the men from Jerusalem. He was interested in Jerusalem, so he asked questions. What are *you* interested in? What causes you ask to questions? What is your burden? What do you like to read and study?

The first indication Nehemiah was pursuing his life purpose, without even knowing it, was that he was simply asking probing questions about a special interest he had. The real indicator of his purpose is found in the next verse:

> When I heard these things, I sat down and wept.
> For some days I mourned and fasted and prayed
> before the God of heaven (Nehemiah 1:4).

When Nehemiah heard the report about the poor conditions in Jerusalem, he cried. What makes you angry, what moves you to fast and call out to the God of heaven, and what makes you weep are often indications of your purpose. I'm sure others heard the same report about Jerusalem that Nehemiah heard, but none of the others were moved as he was. You see, his purpose was to rebuild the city of his fathers, which he did by first rebuilding the walls and then repopulating the city.

You may not know your purpose yet because the situation that will release and define your purpose isn't ready to receive you. Maybe you will rebuild something that isn't yet in need of repair. Or perhaps you will invent something but the technology for your invention isn't quite in place yet. Maybe you will save something or someone who isn't even lost at this time.

That doesn't mean you can't be preparing. Nehemiah was serving the king. You don't serve the king unless you're good at what you do. It's safe to assume Nehemiah was committed to excellence and producing superior work. When you don't know your purpose, pursuing excellence is always a good way to prepare.

I encourage you to spend some time trying to answer

the questions I've raised in this study. Identify what makes you cry or become angry. Reassess your commitment to excellence and make sure it's where it needs to be. Be willing to pay any price to find and fulfill your purpose, even if you're still searching for what it is. If you'll do that, then a situation will present itself to you just as it did to Nehemiah. At that point, all that you've been through will suddenly make sense.

STUDY #28
CHILDREN, PARENTS, AND PURPOSE

I had the privilege of attending a Billy Graham Crusade in Dallas one time. There's no greater example of someone fulfilling his life purpose than Billy Graham. Dr. Graham conducted crusades for over 50 years and changed the world by repeatedly doing what he did best.

I wonder whether Billy Graham's parents saw their son's life purpose. I ask because I have been thinking about Moses and his parents. "At that time Moses was born, and he was no ordinary child. For three months he was cared for in his father's house" (Acts 7:20). What did Moses' parents see that enabled them to recognize their son was not ordinary?

When our son was born, his nose was flat against his face. His hair was standing straight up, even though it was wet. Not only that, but his ears stood out and he was various shades of red, purple, and pink all over his little body. When the nurse handed him to his mother, she looked and him and said, "Maybe he'll be intelligent!" (I'm glad to report that he has grown to be an intelligent *and* handsome adult!)

I think Moses' parents looked at him and saw his purpose. At the time of Moses' birth, Pharaoh ordered all male babies to be thrown into the river. Moses' parents didn't throw him in, however, at least not right away. They cared for and hid him for three months; then complied with Pharaoh's orders. When they did, they put him in a basket first. You know the rest: Pharaoh's daughter found Moses and raised him as her own.

Because his parents saw his purpose, Moses was able to know it as well, probably at an early age. We read:

> He saw one of them being mistreated by an Egyptian, so he went to his defense and avenged him by killing the Egyptian. Moses thought that his own people would realize that God was using him to rescue them, but they did not (Acts 7:24-25).

Moses knew he was to rescue Israel, but there were two problems: Israel didn't recognize his purpose and Moses tried to fulfill it in his own strength by killing Egyptians. What a long road he had to go, killing one Egyptian at a time. He probably said to himself, "One down, three million to go!" Later, after 40 years in the wilderness, Moses rescued Israel, not with a sword, but with his shepherd's staff.

Just as Moses' parents saw his purpose, parents today still have the ability and responsibility to do the same for their children. Our daughter obtained a wonderful job with a great company because she is a gifted salesperson. We saw that gift when she was only four years old. We tried to keep it before her as she went through university and now she is operating in her purpose. A parent plays a big part in directing children in the way they ought to go as determined by their purpose. What do you see in your children? What makes them extraordinary in the sight of God and men?

When we can't see purpose for ourselves, often there are others that clearly see our purpose, just as we can do for our children. We need to seek the advice and input of trusted advisers and use them as a guide to find our way home to our life purpose.

And finally, there's no minimum age to know your purpose. Moses, Samuel, David, and Joseph, just to name a few, all knew their life purpose when they were young. A young person can know their purpose, and no one should discount what they're seeing, no matter how young the person seeing it may be.

I trust that you will apply this insight to your life and the lives of your children, friends, and associates. Look to see what makes these people extraordinary and maybe one of them will take their place on the world's stage, just as Billy Graham did. There are no age restrictions when it comes to purpose.

STUDY #29
KNOWING THE WILL OF GOD

I'm impressed with how many people write me, concerned about "missing the Lord." They want to do God's will and find their purpose, but they don't want to do or say the wrong thing.

Consequently, some are so concerned about "missing the Lord" that they may be "missing the Lord." If your fear of doing the wrong thing leads you to do nothing, then your faith does not have a way to express itself. James wrote, "In the same way, faith by itself, if it is not accompanied by action, is dead" (James 2:17). And without faith, it is impossible to please God (see Hebrews 11:6).

You need to have confidence in the God to whom you pray. Your ability to be heard and receive an answer does not depend on your prayer but on the faithfulness of the God to whom you pray. There's no correct or incorrect formula when you talk to God. You talk and He listens. And then He answers. Let's look at two important passages that highlight this point. The first is found in Luke 11:9-13:

> So I say to you: "Ask and it will be given to you; seek and you will find; knock and the door will be opened to you. For everyone who asks receives; he who seeks finds; and to him who knocks, the door will be opened. Which of you fathers, if your son asks for a fish, will give him a

snake instead? Or if he asks for an egg, will give him a scorpion? If you then, though you are evil, know how to give good gifts to your children, how much more will your Father in heaven give the Holy Spirit to those who ask him!"

If you ask the Father to help you find your purpose, He will hear you. He isn't going to trick you or send you a misleading message. He's your Father, and He will give you what you ask. If you ask God to know and do His will and then think about writing a book, that probably isn't your idea. It's God answering your prayer!

The second verse is in John 7:17. The Pharisees were asking whether Jesus was sent from the Father or not. And Jesus replied by saying, "If any man is willing to do His will, he shall know of the teaching, whether it is of God, or [whether] I speak from Myself" (NAS). Often, the key to finding the will of God for your life is to make a commitment to do it before you know what it is. In essence, Jesus said to the Pharisees, "If you set your will to do God's will, you will always know what His will is!" You may say that it isn't that simple, but I maintain that it is.

How does this apply to purpose and productivity? If you have prayed, God has heard you. You don't have to worry about "missing His will." You must act in faith on what you think you have received. St. Augustine once said, "I pray and then I do what I want." St. Augustine wasn't advocating self-will; he was just confident that the God to whom He prayed was able to shape his will in response to prayer.

I want you to ask God for something you don't know or understand. Maybe you need to find your purpose or want to set a godly goal you can work toward. Before you have the answer, I want you to commit to do or say whatever He shows you before you know what it is! Then I want you to have faith your Father isn't going to trick you and give you a stone instead of the bread for which you are asking. Don't be concerned about "missing God," but be ready to find and do His will. I am confident the God to whom you pray will help you as you seek purposeful direction.

STUDY #30
TOXIC RELATIONSHIPS

I enjoy studying the lives of two men in the Old Testament: David and Jonathan. David and Jonathan were more than friends; they were covenant brothers. They had a special relationship and recognized this relationship by making a special covenant as you see in 1 Samuel 18. Later, when David was avoiding Jonathan's father, King Saul, Jonathan uttered these remarkable words:

> "Don't be afraid," he said. "My father Saul will not lay a hand on you. You will be king over Israel, and I will be second to you. Even my father Saul knows this." The two of them made a covenant before the Lord. Then Jonathan went home, but David remained at Horesh (1 Samuel 23:17-18).

Why are these words so remarkable? Jonathan was the king's son, the heir apparent and the second in command. Here, he acknowledged that David's purpose was to be king, and his purpose was to serve David as his right-hand man. Jonathan relinquished his claim to the throne and expressed his willingness to accept the purpose God had for him.

Even though Jonathan knew this and spoke about it, however, it never came to pass. Jonathan died in battle with his father: "The Philistines pressed hard after Saul and his sons, and they killed his sons Jonathan, Abinadab and Malki-Shua" (1 Samuel 31:2). I have a question to ask you. With the knowledge Jonathan had, what was he doing with his worthless father, going into a battle that could not be won? Because Jonathan could not deal with his father, he forfeited his right to fulfill his purpose. He died and David mourned him for the rest of his life. Saul had become a toxic relationship where Jonathan's purpose was concerned.

What does this have to do with you and me? It's important that we follow God's will for our lives and not let relationships hinder us. We can't allow our supervisor, pastor, friends or family hinder us from pursuing and fulfilling our purpose. No matter how tough the situation, we must steward our purpose. We must oversee it and not allow anyone to talk us out of it or keep us from being the fullest, best expression of who God created us to be.

You need to take an honest look at your life and purpose. Have you listened to a negative, discouraging, toxic report from someone about you and your abilities? Have you put your purpose on the shelf to please or serve someone else? Have you spent time trying to tell God why you aren't the one to do what it is that is in your heart? As you answer these questions, please remember Jonathan. Jonathan knew his purpose but lost it because he could not admit that his father was a toxic scoundrel who did not have anyone's best interests at heart but his own. You'll only answer to God for the results of what He has assigned you to do. I urge you to determine in your heart to make pleasing Him your top priority, even at the risk of disappointing someone you love.

STUDY #31
NANCY'S STORY

Several months ago, I was teaching a seminar and thought about my friend Nancy. I wanted to share with them the impact one of my first purpose seminars had on her and felt I needed to make sure I had her story correct. Through a mutual friend, I contacted Nancy and asked her to write about what has happened in her life the last 12 years. Here's her reply:

> I remember hearing you teach on purpose in your *Life is a Goldmine: Can You Dig It?* seminar. At that time, I was at a critical point in my faith journey. I ached for more creative expression in my life. Being the daughter of the sports editor for our local paper, writing came naturally and easy for me. I loved words and I had always loved music. Little did I realize that your seminar would be one of the things God would use to help me find the courage to believe and pursue the desires of my heart, namely songwriting. First, I had to acknowledge the desire that I wanted to write to myself, to God, and to family and friends. Then I began to actively pursue this dream and desire one day at a time, one step at a time. I remember the phrase "never despise small beginnings." Maybe I heard it from you.

Now, some years later, I have published more than 300 songs, written 12 musicals (children and adult), have had four songs nominated for a Dove Award, and created the children's praise character Miss PattyCake. The Miss PattyCake line how has 6 videos and 2 CD's, which I helped to write and create. I just finished my first book, to be published and released in March, which will be *A Miss PattyCake Easter Story.*

As a speaker, writer, worship leader, and a creative consultant, I desire to increase my speaking venues and to write several books. I now have my own publishing company, Mother's Heart Music and Mother's Heart Ministries. They both exist to nurture, inspire, and encourage all people to experience and know the love of God.

You would have to know Nancy to fully appreciate this report. She is neither wealthy, nor is she "well connected" in the music industry. (I write this because often we put successful people in a special category and lose the encouragement they can be for us.) She is a "regular person" like you and me who decided one day to step out "to actively pursue this dream and desire, one day at a time, one step at a time." She gave God something to bless and He did. And the exciting thing is that she isn't finished. God has more for her to do and she is still young (well, she's around my age, which is looking younger all the time!).

Like Nancy, your journey can begin right now. And your journey will start where hers did when you acknowledge to yourself, to God, and to others what it is that you want and were created to do. They may laugh, yawn or misunderstand. Their reaction (or lack of it) isn't important because you're not saying it for them. You're saying it for you and for God who put that dream in you in the first place.

And you're saying it to release the dynamic of a spoken vision as outlined in these passages:

> Surely then you will find delight in the Almighty and will lift up your face to God. You will pray to him, and he will hear you, and you will fulfill your vows. What you decide on will be done, and light will shine on your ways. When men are brought low and you say, "Lift them up!" then he will save the downcast. He will deliver even one who is not innocent, who will be delivered through the cleanness of your hands (Job 22:26-30).

If you don't have anyone else to tell, then write and tell me. Just tell someone, and then, remembering Nancy's story, get started creating your own.

STUDY #32
OPPOSITION

I was reflecting on the Christmas story and how much turmoil Jesus' birth caused. Consider Mary, who became pregnant outside of marriage, or so Joseph and her family thought. We see Joseph, who was ready to divorce Mary until the angel appeared and told him to do otherwise. We see Mary making a trip on foot and by donkey to Bethlehem while she was nine months pregnant. When she arrived, she had to give birth in an outdoor stable. Later, King Herod, who heard about Jesus and perceived that He was a threat to his throne, had all the male children two years or younger killed in Bethlehem. Yes, the birth of Jesus wasn't exactly the best of times for those closely involved.

That's how tough things can get when you function in your purpose. Until you clarify your purpose, life can be peaceful, perhaps uneventful. Once you set out on a course to fulfill your purpose, however, all heaven and some of hell can break loose. You may even find that you have enemies simply because you are trying to do what you were created to do.

In the book of Genesis, Joseph wasn't popular with his brothers, but after he had his dreams that his purpose would be to rule over them, they conspired to kill him. Moses was successful in Egypt until he began to rescue his people. Then Egypt and Pharaoh became his enemies.

David was a shepherd boy who became a popular and successful servant of King Saul. After David was anointed to be king (his purpose), Saul persecuted him. In the New Testament, a man named Saul was a successful Jewish evangelist and theologian until his fateful trip on the Damascus road. After that, Jews, and even some of his fellow believers, became a source of suffering and pain.

Then there was Jesus. He stirred up some enemies at birth and then seemed to settle into a simple lifestyle in Nazareth for the next 30 years. When He began to fulfill His purpose to seek and save the lost, He found many ready to oppose and even kill Him. Are you seeing a pattern here? Your purpose can produce circumstances that are painful and even dangerous. If you understand this, you'll see that the opposition is a confirmation that you're doing something right, not something wrong. Your purpose is so powerful that it will usually threaten someone, maybe even someone close to you, someone from whom you would not expect such opposition.

I urge you to spend a few minutes reflecting on the price that Jesus paid for you to enjoy what you have. Then I hope you will resolve to be a man or woman of purpose, to be a person who will see your enemies and opponents for what they are: a confirmation of the correct path you are pursuing. If you're encountering opposition, have hope! If you're afraid to embrace your purpose because it may make someone unhappy, take courage! If Joseph, Moses, David, Paul, and Jesus had enemies, you will too. They made their purpose their life, and the rest is history. I trust you will join them and make some history of your own.

STUDY #33
ENJOY YOUR WORK

Let's look at a familiar passage in Ecclesiastes 3:1-13:

There is a time for everything, and a season for every activity under heaven: a time to be born and a time to die, a time to plant and a time to uproot, a time to kill and a time to heal, a time to tear down and a time to build, a time to weep and a time to laugh, a time to mourn and a time to dance, a time to scatter stones and a time to gather them, a time to embrace and a time to refrain, a time to search and a time to give up, a time to keep and a time to throw away, a time to tear and a time to mend, a time to be silent and a time to speak, a time to love and a time to hate, a time for war and a time for peace. What does the worker gain from his toil? I have seen the burden God has laid on men. He has made everything beautiful in its time. He has also set eternity in the hearts of men; yet they cannot fathom what God has done from beginning to end. I know that there is nothing better for men than to be happy and do good while they live. That everyone may eat and drink, and find satisfaction in all his toil—this is the gift of God.

Do you have satisfaction in your work? If not, then perhaps the reason for your dissatisfaction can be found in verse two, which states that there is a time to be born and a time to die. The key to your satisfaction may be in not trying to keep something alive but in seeing something die, even something that has become special to you.

It's hard to discern the seasons of life and work in which you find yourself. Something that began with such hope and energy may now be taking from you the very life that it once gave. I regularly receive emails from people who were trying to fit 28 hours of work into a 24-hour day. There's just no way to do that. I encourage each person who writes to find what it is they need to stop doing and then focus on what needs to be done.

Activities, roles, and even businesses, ministries, and churches have a time to be born and then have a time to die. That's a part of the life cycle. Trying to keep something alive that is past its season of life is not only counterproductive, but also impossible. If you are like many people, you may regularly set goals and resolutions. If those resolutions have any chance of being fulfilled, something else may have to come to an end before it can begin.

This isn't easy to do. It's not easy to end something that still has life and that you still enjoy doing. If you want to be purposeful and productive, you must regularly determine what stage or season your activities are in. Should they continue or should they end so new activities or direction can emerge in the coming days? All I can say as I face this process is "His will be done." I pray the same for you.

STUDY #34
FLAVORED WATER

Jesus said: "Whoever believes in me, as the Scripture has said, streams of living water will flow from within him. By this he meant the Spirit, whom those who believed in him were later to receive" (John 7:38-39). If you have faith in Jesus, He promised something would come from you like a river or streams of living water that has life for you and others. In other words, Jesus promised you would be in a flow of life that would sustain you and others around you.

The waters that flow from you, while coming from the Spirit's presence, will have *your* flavor. Those waters should "taste" like you; they should have the taste of your experience, gifts, and purpose. Many people, in trying to be spiritual, distance themselves from who they are and try to be someone they are not. God made you as you are and comes into your life not to radically change you but to make the fullest, best expression of who He intended for you to be in the first place.

When you sing, the Spirit may be flowing from you, but it's *your* voice. When you counsel, the Spirit may be using you to help someone, but you're doing it utilizing *your* style and counseling technique. Even the writers of the gospels, who were writing the inspired word of God, used words, phrases, and grammatical styles unique to them.

The water that flowed out of them tasted like them, but it has brought the Spirit's life to many throughout the ages.

The water that comes from you and me must not be artificially flavored. We don't have to be like someone else to fulfill our purpose or to please God. We are free to be us, to find a flow of life and purpose that comes naturally and touches others. We don't have to try and eliminate all flavor from our water. God is working in and through us for His good pleasure.

If you love music, then love it with all your heart and allow God to use that love to flavor your water. If you're a businessperson, then let the flavor of commerce or sales be what people taste when they "drink" from you.

Now there are some tastes that you must work to keep out of your flowing streams. First, there must not be any salt in your water (see James 3:12) that comes from cursing or gossiping. And there must not be any bitter taste in your water from grumbling or complaining about your circumstances (see Exodus 15:23). And, of course, there must not be any poison in your water that comes from sin or unresolved issues of the past (see Numbers 5:22-27). Apart from these things that can taint your water, you and I are to let the rivers flow, rivers of purpose that God will use to water our families, our nations, and even the world.

Sometimes we can be ambivalent about our flavor. We can feel that we aren't dynamic or exciting enough to be productive. You can be biased toward your own creativity and personality. When that happens, you'll work to restrict your flow because you don't think you have anything worth giving out to the world. I know that part of what I do is to help people remove the restrictions to their flow. Many people have told me, "Your message is so liberating! I feel free to be who I have been all along."

Is there water flowing from you, and does it taste like you? Have you "dammed up" the flow due to fear, confusion, or doubt? What flavor are you? Are your waters vintage you, or have they been injected by the taste of someone else or of elements that make the water undrinkable? I hope you will determine to have faith and let your rivers flow. Be yourself and let your purpose flavor the water of life that comes from you. If you taste good to God, why would you want to change?

STUDY #35
COURAGE

When I talk with people, trying to help them clarify their purpose, I usually ask them one question: What are you afraid of? It's the question I would ask you in this essay. Don't be too quick to answer as we examine this question together. In fact, you may want to take a minute and list four of five things that come to mind as you try to face your fears.

When I first decided to develop the *Seven Steps of a PurposeQuest* seminar, I was excited and anxious. In the three months it took to develop, I believe I faced just about every fear possible. What if no one comes? What if the weather is bad? What if the material isn't relevant? What if no one comes? What if I lose money? What if no one comes? (You can tell that my greatest fear was that no one would come!)

Someone once told me that courage isn't action in the absence of fear; it's action in the presence of fear. As I've studied fear, I came across an interesting Bible verse:

> But the cowardly [fearful], the unbelieving, the vile, the murderers, the sexually immoral, those who practice magic arts, the idolaters and all liars—their place will be in the fiery lake of burning sulfur. This is the second death (Revelation 21:8).

I can see why most of those listed end up in the fiery lake, but I was surprised to find the cowardly there. It seems that inaction due to unbelief or fear of failure is more serious in God's sight than I had previously considered it to be.

I've played enough sports to know that you can't perform while you're afraid. You just simply must play and let your instincts take over. If you must think about what you're doing, then usually you won't be effective on the field. You practice honing your skills, but then you let it all flow in the game. There are many people who can't "flow" because they're afraid. Are you one of those people?

Now back to the question at hand: What are you afraid of? Fear can paralyze you and cause you to put off what you should be doing. In other words, fear can cause you to be disobedient. Face your fears and then take some step to do something you've wanted but have been afraid to do. Don't wait for your fear to go away, but admit it, and despite it, I want you to write the letter, make the phone call, talk to your supervisor or pastor, or make plans to do something bold. Make these coming days ones of courage and act on your dreams and purpose. As you do, you will join the army of God where only the courageous action in faith will bring victory.

STUDY #36
SMALL IS GOOD

One of my purpose heroes is George Washington Carver, the famous African American scientist who lived in the period following the American Civil War. At a time when Americans of color suffered unspeakable conditions and prejudice, Carver single-handedly revolutionized agriculture in the American South, and he did it through work and prayer.

From his platform at Tuskegee Institute in Alabama, Carver urged farmers to plant peanuts, having discovered that peanuts were a perfect crop for the southern soil and climate. There was only one problem: at that time there was no market for peanuts! Farmers were angry and Carver was embarrassed. George Washington Carver prayed, and God gave him the solution to his problem.

The story has it that Carver began his prayer by asking, "Oh Lord, teach me about the universe," to which the Lord responded, "That is too much for you." Then Carver prayed, "Then Lord, teach me about man." Again the Lord responded, "You are still thinking too big." Finally, Carver cried out, "Lord, then please teach me about the peanut!" From that prayer, Carver went back to his simple laboratory and discovered more than 300 uses for the peanut over the course of his illustrious career. He found ways to make fertilizer, paint, and glue from peanuts and discovered peanut oil and peanut butter. While he was at it, he also discovered more than 100 uses for sweet potatoes.

The lessons from Carver's life for you and me are basic. First, prayer works. If you need wisdom or insight, why not ask God for it? Second, you need to keep things small. You don't need to think about changing the world to serve God; you just need to think about how to change *your* world. Armed with the knowledge of your purpose and prayer, you can discover a significant breakthrough that will touch a few or many. You may be able to take what seems like a simple interest and turn it into a historic career, just like George Washington Carver did. Third, there are many discoveries yet to be made. Why can't you and I be the ones who discover them?

Ask God for wisdom concerning the interests you have, no matter how small or simple they may seem to be. And then expect God to answer you. Be ready to learn new things about the seemingly small interests in your life and then yield them to God. From that, there's no telling what God can do with you and through you!

STUDY #37
PURPOSE PAIN

Suffering and difficulty seem to be necessary factors in anyone's quest for their purpose. Pain adds a dimension of maturity and reality that makes us stronger and more sensitive to the needs around us. It was written of Jesus: "He learned obedience from what he suffered" (Hebrews 5:8). If that's how Jesus learned obedience, you can be sure that we will learn the same way.

The Bible is full of stories of purposeful people who suffered and waited. Moses spent 40 years in the wilderness before he returned to Egypt to rescue his people. After Samuel had anointed him to be the new king, David spent 25 years waiting to replace the existing one. Joseph's story in the Old Testament is special to me. (Take the time to read his story for yourself in Genesis 37-50.)

I won't go into the entire story, but Joseph suffered for 22 years at the hands of family and associates to fulfill his purpose. Then he had to fulfill it in a foreign land under difficult circumstances. Things were so difficult that he named his second son "Ephraim," which means "God has made me fruitful in the land of my suffering."

Sometimes the suffering is in not being able to immediately fulfill your purpose once you find it. Another key source of suffering is the opposition that often comes from people close to you. Finally, you may suffer through some failure, having started out confident of success. Whatever the source of your pain, it is part of everyone's quest for their purpose. The pain will help you grow and deal with any pride; it will also connect you to the pain of others.

Are you in a difficult place? Then you're probably right where you need to be! You may want to study some historical person of purpose. What role did suffering have in their life? What role is it playing in your own life? God can still make you fruitful amid your own land of suffering. I pray that your pain will lead to purpose and productivity, and that it won't last one day longer than it needs to last.

STUDY #38
NEVER TOO YOUNG

I've found that this generation of youth "connects" with the purpose message in a meaningful way. In Zimbabwe, one young lady came to the *Seven Steps* seminar and went home to begin writing a children's devotional. Other parents reported how their children went home and laid out plans to find their purpose, to the surprise and delight of their parents. I use my own daughter as another example. Since she was four, Deborah could sell anything. She usually outsold her classmates when her school had fundraising projects, and as a teenager, she got a job with Sears and Roebuck as a telemarketer. She won a district award from Sears for her work, even though she was only fifteen.

When she entered college, her mother and I were surprised that Deborah chose education as her major. After being in school for only a few weeks, she called home and told me that she had a "vision." As she was entering the people mover at her university, she "saw" herself getting on a plane. Deborah said she knew she was getting on that plane to go sell something to someone. She got off the people mover and transferred into the business school. When Deborah graduated, she went to work for a pharmaceutical company as a sales rep. They gave her a company car and generous benefits. My daughter is a young woman of purpose, and she doesn't have to suffer in the wrong job to find her way to fulfillment.

Recently I talked to a group of youth in England about purpose. I showed them, from the Bible, how many children and young people knew their purpose early in life. Joseph knew at 17 years of age that he would be the leader of his father's household. Samuel heard God's call when he was a child serving with Eli. David was a teenager when Samuel anointed him king of Israel. Daniel was a youth when he entered the service of the king of Babylon. And Mary, mother of Jesus, had an angel visit her while she was a teenager and change her life forever.

What does this have to do with you? If you have children or work with young people, talk to them about purpose and see how they respond. See if they don't readily connect with what you're saying. If you aren't numbered among the youth anymore, there's still hope. Jesus urged us all to be like children as we seek to enter His kingdom. Try to reconnect with your youthful ability to dream, to think about what you want to do in the future. Don't talk yourself out of it, but act like a child and live in that dream today. Then when you "wake up" from your dream, see what steps you can take to make that dream a reality.

Purpose is a hot topic in church and business circles. Many authors are writing, "You have a purpose…you have a purpose." When asked in return, "What is my purpose?" most respond, "You have a purpose." They can't really say anything more specific than that. My goal is to enlist an army of purposeful people who not only know their purpose but can also help others find their purpose. If you haven't already, I invite you to enlist in this purpose army, whether you're young or young at heart.

STUDY #39
GOD WANTS MORE

It's interesting to study how Jesus used parables when He taught. Parables are stories with a moral or lesson, and there are 41 parables that are recorded in the first three gospels. I'm especially intrigued by the story found in Matthew 25:14-30. You may want to read the entire story, for I include only the last few verses here:

> Then the man who had received the one talent came. "Master," he said, "I knew that you are a hard man, harvesting where you have not sown and gathering where you have not scattered seed. So I was afraid and went out and hid your talent in the ground. See, here is what belongs to you." His master replied, "You wicked, lazy servant! So you knew that I harvest where I have not sown and gather where I have not scattered seed? Well then, you should have put my money on deposit with the bankers, so that when I returned I would have received it back with interest. Take the talent from him and give it to the one who has the ten talents. For everyone who has will be given more, and he will have an abundance. Whoever does not have, even what he has will be taken from him. And throw that worthless servant outside, into the darkness, where there

will be weeping and gnashing of teeth" (Matthew 25:24-30).

The talents referred to here were monetary units and not gifts or abilities, so the three men in the parable received decreasing amounts of money. The master expected each of them to bring unspecified increase to what they were given. The first two did just that; the third man did not.

When the day of accounting came, the third man who did not manage to obtain any increase told the master why. He said that he was angry and afraid. Perhaps he was upset because the other two men got more money to work with than he did. The servant saw the master as a tyrant, expecting increase for which the master himself didn't labor. The servant took and hid the money and gave it back undiminished, unharmed, but without any increase. Upon hearing how difficult he was to work with, the master became angry and ordered the one talent to be taken away from the servant and given to the servant who had earned the largest increase.

This is the story of many people with whom I work. They are afraid of failure and would rather do nothing than the wrong thing. They play it safe and hope to not lose rather than to win. Here is a quote from Simon Kistemaker's book entitled *The Parables*:

> The servant entrusted with the one talent kept the deposit safely in a hidden place. He feared to put it to use, for he knew that his master would demand the talent from him upon his return. Fear, therefore, completely overshadowed love, trust, and faith. Fear is the opposite of confidence.
>
> The Christian who puts faith to work will reap immense dividends. He is not concerned about himself and his own interests, for whatever he owns belongs to the Lord and whatever he does he does for the Lord. No follower of Jesus can

ever say that he lacks the gifts to be of service simply because he is not a Paul, Luther, Calvin, or Knox. The parable teaches that every servant has received gifts, "each according to his ability." Jesus knows the capability of every Christian, and he expects an increase.

As with many other parables, specific details cannot and should not be stressed and applied. Rather, the central message of faithfulness is important. The parable of the talents teaches that every believer has been endowed with gifts differing according to ability, and that these gifts must be put to use in God's service. In the kingdom of God everyone is expected to employ fully the gifts he has received. In God's kingdom there simply is no room for drones—only for worker bees.[12]

Which of the servants are you? Are you working in faith to bring increase to your world through your purpose and dreams, or are you afraid and hesitant? I trust that you will work hard to bring the faithful increase that is your right and duty as a follower of Jesus. After all, increase is your duty and, what's more, God's expectation.

STUDY #40
JUST AND ONLY

Let's look at the man named Nehemiah in the next few studies. If you remember from an earlier study, Nehemiah was an Old Testament builder and leader. When we read about Nehemiah, we learn that he was the cupbearer for the king in a land far from his home. Nehemiah says,

> Hanani, one of my brothers, came from Judah with some other men, and I questioned them about the Jewish remnant that survived the exile, and also about Jerusalem. They said to me, "Those who survived the exile and are back in the province are in great trouble and disgrace. The wall of Jerusalem is broken down, and its gates have been burned with fire." When I heard these things, I sat down and wept. For some days I mourned and fasted and prayed before the God of heaven (Nehemiah 1:2-4).

I'm not sure if Nehemiah realized that this visitor from his homeland would hold the key to Nehemiah's purpose. You may be searching for your purpose, but it may not be clear because history hasn't made it clear. Nehemiah couldn't know his purpose until Jerusalem was in disrepair and the people were in desperate straits. One day, a man appeared who gave Nehemiah a bad report about the condition of Jerusalem. This report, probably heard by many others, impacted Nehemiah more deeply than anyone else. This is like Winston Churchill, who was a politician all his life, but who didn't find his purpose until Nazi Germany threatened the world. It was then Churchill realized he had been born to save the Western world from the Nazis.

Notice how Nehemiah went about seeking clarification of his purpose. He stopped what he was doing and sat down. He cried, almost always a sure sign that someone is considering or close to purpose-related activities. Then Nehemiah prayed and even went without food. The issue of purpose is so powerful that it can often make you forget about food. Even Jesus said, "I have food to eat that you know nothing about" (John 4:32).

Then later in the story, Nehemiah went in to see the king. The king noticed that Nehemiah looked glum and said:

> So the king asked me, "Why does your face look so sad when you are not ill? This can be nothing but sadness of heart." I was very much afraid, but I said to the king, "May the king live forever! Why should my face not look sad when the city where my fathers are buried lies in ruins, and its gates have been destroyed by fire?" The king said to me, "What is it you want?" Then I prayed to the God of heaven, and I answered the king, "If it pleases the king and if your servant has found favor in his sight, let him send me to the city in Judah where my fathers are buried so that I can rebuild it" (Nehemiah 2:2-5).

It's important that you be ready to describe your purpose in one short, concise statement. If a king asks you what it is that you want, you shouldn't respond, "Well, uh, I sort of would like to, you know, well, I was hoping that I could, like maybe go to the mission field." Many people are so uncomfortable talking about themselves that they miss opportunities because they aren't clear or they're afraid to be specific. Not so with Nehemiah. He asked God for help and then he stated his purpose clearly: "Send me to the city in Judah where my fathers are buried so that I can rebuild it."

When I sit and help someone clarify their purpose, I try to listen carefully. Two words seem to occur regularly when people talk to me about purpose. They tell me that they "just" do this or "only" do that. "Just" and "only" are often gateways to a clear purpose statement, for we often look past the obvious in search of a more glamorous or dramatic purpose.

Nehemiah prayed for clarity and then he told the king, his supervisor, what he wanted to do. The king was inclined to help him. Make every effort to be clear and direct in your description of who you are and what you were created to do. If someone who has the power to help you fulfill your purpose asks, be ready to tell them what you need without apology. See the words "just" and "only" as keys to your life purpose and then you'll see that what you "only" do has the power to change your life and world.

STUDY #41
HANDLING CRITICISM

I've written about purpose and opposition before, but I learned some things from Nehemiah's life that may help you in your own search for purpose. As we saw in the previous study, Nehemiah was deeply moved by the poor conditions of his home city. After he fasted and prayed, he was able to clearly declare what he wanted to do while talking to his supervisor, the king. The king gave Nehemiah a leave of absence to go to Jerusalem, rebuild the walls, and resettle the inhabitants.

This is where his opposition appeared. There were people who had a vested interest in Jerusalem not being re-built, and they began to make life difficult for Nehemiah and his workers. I find it fascinating that often there's no opposition in your life until you start to fulfill your purpose as we saw earlier in the life of Joseph. Family, friends, church members, and coworkers—the people who know you best—then may tell you that you're crazy or misguided. They may even become actively involved in opposing the steps you are taking to fulfill your purpose.

Nehemiah's enemies used three tactics to keep him from his purpose: intimidation, confrontation, and criti-cism. Let's look at the criticism that came his way:

1. *They said he was rebellious.* "But when Sanballat the Horonite, Tobiah the Ammonite official, and Geshem

the Arab heard about it, they mocked and ridiculed us. 'What is this you are doing?' they asked. 'Are you rebelling against the king?'" (Nehemiah 2:19). Often your efforts to fulfill your purpose are seen as going against someone else's plans for you. They will then accuse you of trying to do your "own thing" and portray you as an independent or a loner.

2. *They said the job was too big for Nehemiah.* "When Sanballat heard that we were rebuilding the wall, he became angry and was greatly incensed. He ridiculed the Jews, and in the presence of his associates and the army of Samaria, he said, 'What are those feeble Jews doing? Will they restore their wall? Will they offer sacrifices? Will they finish in a day? Can they bring the stones back to life from those heaps of rubble-burned as they are?'" (Nehemiah 4:1-2). Sometimes people get angry for no reason as you travel the road of your purpose. They try to tell you what you want to do is impossible and no one has ever done it before.

3. *They said he was not capable.* "Tobiah the Ammonite, who was at his side, said, 'What they are building—if even a fox climbed up on it, he would break down their wall of stones!'" (Nehemiah 4:3). Some people will tell you you're not that good or talented, that you don't have what it takes to make it in music, theater, business, ministry, missions, or any other field of endeavor that you desire to pursue.

Nehemiah learned to deal with his critics, and you'll need to learn to do that too if you're to succeed in fulfilling your purpose. Paul wrote something that encourages me:

> Am I now trying to win the approval of men, or of God? Or am I trying to please men? If I were still trying to please men, I would not be a servant of Christ (Galatians 1:10).

Your purpose is the will of God for your life. You don't need anyone's permission to do God's will; but in doing His will, you will encounter opposition and criticism. You must learn to deal with it and move on, for anyone who has done great things has had to do the same.

I trust that you will work for the praise of God and not let your opposition hinder you, not even the opposition from within. There are times when there's an internal critic that accuses you of the same three things that are outlined above. I urge you to move beyond external and internal criticism to take purposeful action in your life. Listen to your critics but don't take them too seriously. What God thinks is the only thing that matters at the end of the day.

STUDY #42
HE CHANGED THE "S" TO "P"

I read a great book, entitled *Paul: The Traveler and Roman Citizen*, by William Ramsey. I love to read anything about the Apostle Paul because he was such a man of purpose. Paul was difficult to work with and had little patience for underachievers. Next to Jesus, however, no one played a greater role in the development of the early church than Paul. He was able to do so, not because he was smart (he was) or aggressive (he was), but because he was a man of purpose. When he went to the Gentiles, God went with him and the results were spectacular.

I was reading about Paul's first missionary journey to Cyprus and the Galatian region in Acts 13. When Paul confronted a magician who was trying to hinder his work, Luke (the writer of Acts) stated, "Then Saul, who was also called Paul . . ." (Acts 13:9). What a simple but powerful statement! It was 14 years since Saul had his dramatic encounter with Jesus on the Damascus road and then he stepped forward on the mission field and said, "My name is no longer Saul but Paul." It took Paul 14 years to realize who he was and what he was created to do, and when he did, he accepted his name change to Paul.

Think about it. Saul was a Roman citizen from the cross-cultural city of Tarsus. He knew four languages. Saul understood the Roman/Greek world of his day, and he was in some ways more comfortable in the Gentile world than he was in Jerusalem. Saul had legal rights as a Roman citizen—rights that Jesus did not have when He was crucified. Saul was a Jew *and* a Roman! In Cyprus, Saul stepped forward into his purpose e and from that point, he was known, and is still known today, as Paul. What a difference a one letter change from "S" to "P" made in world history!

That's the power of purpose. Nothing changed in Saul's life except how he saw himself in his mind. That was enough to have him boldly step forward and in essence say, "This is who I am. This is what I was created to do and be." From that point, his travels, letters and legacy have impacted the world for 2,000 years.

Who are you? What is your "name"? Are you ready to step forward and acknowledge who you are and what your past has shaped and prepared you to be today? Are you prepared to stop identifying with how others see you and make a statement of purpose for yourself? Now is the time to step out of the shadows of who you have been into the light of who God wants you to be. The world is waiting for the real you to emerge, and you may not have to do a lot to make that happen. After all, Paul simply accepted one letter change in his name and the rest is history. What little thing can you do that will enable you to embrace who you are? What are you waiting for?

STUDY #43
STOP TRYING TO FIGURE IT OUT

When I talk with people to help clarify their purpose, some are so stuck on one idea in their head they cannot follow what is in their heart. Consequently, their head is helping them see options but isn't helping them choose among them. If this describes where you are, this study is for you!

First and foremost, faith is what you use to find your purpose. When you start looking for your purpose, you must believe that you have one. That requires faith in the God of your purpose and not faith in your ability to figure out what it is. You must have faith that God is able to show you what your purpose is. This sounds so basic, but it's a critical step. I talk to many people who are praying to know their purpose, but they don't really believe that God is showing them what it is. They dismiss the "spiritual" evidence of joy, passion, and talent in the light of their rational understanding of the evidence. If you're praying to know your purpose, why are you so skeptical that God is answering? If you're seeking the mind of Christ, why are you surprised that you may have it? I'm reminded of a simple concept that Jesus taught:

"Which of you fathers, if your son asks for a fish,

will give him a snake instead? Or if he asks for an egg, will give him a scorpion? If you then, though you are evil, know how to give good gifts to your children, how much more will your Father in heaven give the Holy Spirit to those who ask him!" (Luke 11:11-13).

I've known people who ask what their purpose is and then are released from their jobs the next week. That's difficult, but I urge them to see that as an answer to prayer. I've talked to others who prayed and then had a perfect stranger come up to them to give them an important clue in understanding their purpose. Do you expect this to happen to you? If you ask your Father for purpose, do you expect the unexpected? When it comes, will you receive it?

Faith is the means not only to find but also to fulfill your purpose. I talk to people who haven't written a book because they don't know who will publish or purchase their book. Faith requires that you do what you can do and then trust God to do what only He can do. You write, God publishes. You create; God sells. If you stop taking the steps you *can* take because you don't understand how the latter steps can ever happen, you are guilty of trying to figure out how everything will work out. In short, you don't have faith and you're allowing your lack of faith to hinder what you can do today. I can only remind you of one of my favorite verses: "In the same way, faith by itself, if it is not accompanied by action, is dead" (James 2:17).

If you don't take the steps only *you* can take, don't expect God to take the steps only *He* can take. In many ways, how God responds to you is determined by how you respond to God. I hope this will help you to stop trying to figure out what to do and to just do it. I hope this will also help you see what is happening in your life as an answer to prayer, an answer that you aren't supposed to analyze but act upon.

STUDY #44
MOSES: "HERE I AM!"

One day, while reading Exodus 3, I noticed that Moses said seven things during his encounter with the Lord at the burning bush. The first thing Moses said to the Lord involved three simple words: "Here I am." Those words may not seem very important, but they are. Let's examine these words more closely and see how they can help you as you walk out your purpose.

I did a quick study of others who said "Here I am" and found out that Abraham said it twice when God spoke to him to sacrifice Isaac (see Genesis 22:1, 7, 11). Then Jacob said it in Genesis 46:2 when God spoke to him to go down to Egypt. Finally, Samuel said it when the Lord called him to a prophetic purpose (see 1 Samuel 3:4). What's so important about these words? I think they're critical to any-one who is on search for their purpose, expecting to hear or see something from God.

"Here I am" signifies that you're ready to do what God wants before you know what it is. It says that you're ready and trust whatever God shows you to do. When you're looking for your purpose, you can't have a "Huh?" attitude. You must have a "Here I am" attitude if you hope to clarify your purpose.

I once knew someone struggling to find their pur-pose, and a pastor gave them good advice. He said, "During your search, can you thank God for your purpose before you know what it is? Can you believe that God will show it to you and say thank you in advance?" I think that advice was "Here I am" advice. You present yourself at attention, just like a good soldier awaiting orders. And then you wait to hear what they are.

As you pursue your purpose, you need to couple a "Here I am" attitude with a "Here I am" faith. Read the passages that are referenced above and study the search of Moses, Jacob and Samuel. Then prepare yourself for the God of your purpose to reveal it. When and how He does that, I can't say. But "Here I am" faith will help make it happen.

STUDY #45
MOSES: "WHO AM I?"

In the previous study, we looked at the first of seven comments that Moses made when he had his encounter with the Lord at the burning bush. We saw that his first comment was, "Here I am," and saw that we need to have a ready attitude to listen and do whatever God wants us to do.

Now let's look at his second comment: "But Moses said to God, 'Who am I, that I should go to Pharaoh and bring the Israelites out of Egypt?'" (Exodus 3:11).

It seems that Moses had something in common with many people, and that was low self-esteem. God had just confirmed to him his purpose, a purpose that he already knew; yet Moses immediately began to tell God why he wasn't the one to go to Egypt. There was a man standing before a burning bush, hearing the voice of God, and he was telling God that he was insignificant. Does this sound familiar? Don't you and I often do the same thing?

We pray to do God's will and fulfill our purpose and then we're surprised when God agrees. When we sense our purpose, we tend to present reasons why we can't do it. We might say, "Who am I, Lord, for I don't have the money, education, experience, permission, or talent to do Your will?"

Are you struggling with low self-esteem or lack of confidence? Then first, you can take consolation that Moses struggled with the same things and still went on to do great things for God. That alone should encourage you to move on and fulfill your purpose. But if you need some additional encouragement, consider these verses:

1. *"As God's fellow workers we urge you not to receive God's grace in vain"* (2 Corinthians 6:1-2). You are not alone. When you work for God, you work with God. He is your co-worker! If it's only you, you may have cause for concern. God is working with you in whatever it is He asks you to do.

2. *"I have been crucified with Christ and I no longer live, but Christ lives in me. The life I live in the body, I live by faith in the Son of God, who loved me and gave himself for me"* (Galatians 2:20-21). More than simply being *with you*, God lives *in you*. You can learn how to surrender to Jesus who lives in you and works through you. That makes you a carrier of Someone special who empowers you to fulfill your purpose.

3. *"But we have the mind of Christ"* (1 Corinthians 2:16). If one of the effects of Christ living in you is to have His mind, why are you so surprised and doubtful that you may have it? When you realize that you have this mind, you will have more confidence in your ability, or rather God's ability to fulfill the task that's before you.

Now is a good time to face your lack of confidence and low self-esteem. Honestly assess where you are regarding God's purpose for your life. If you are thinking or saying, "Who am I?" then it's time to answer that question, relying on truths found in the three verses shown. Move beyond your limitations into the vast possibilities of those people who have stopped putting faith in their own abilities to put their faith in God.

STUDY #46
MOSES: "WHO SENT ME?"

Now let's look at Moses' third comment:

"Suppose I go to the Israelites and say to them, 'The God of your fathers has sent me to you,' and they ask me, 'What is his name?' Then what shall I tell them?" (Exodus 3:13).

I think Moses was stalling for time when he asked this question. He was basically saying, "I'm not ready to go. I don't have all the necessary information. I need to know more about God. I need to be better equipped." I've encountered people doing the same thing when they find their purpose or have an idea. They often tell me, "I'm praying about it," but when I probe, I find out they aren't really. Or they tell me, "I don't have the education," or "I don't pray enough," or "I need to get this fixed or right in my life before I go and do." These are excuses that delay doing what it is that is before us.

I'm not saying that you don't need more training, that you don't need to pray more, or that you don't need to know more about the Lord. None of these issues disqualify you from doing God's will today. Nor do they represent something that can't be addressed *while* you are fulfilling your purpose instead of *before* you fulfill it. Many people are trying to figure out *how* to do God's will before they begin. Seldom is that possible.

Hebrews 11:34-35 states, "Whose weakness was turned to strength; and who became powerful in battle and routed foreign armies." I thought it interesting that the heroes of faith didn't wait until they had strength; rather they received strength *when* they entered the battle. Too many people say, "If God gives me strength, I'll go and do it," but God says, "If you go and do it, I'll give you the strength (or wisdom, power or ability) that you need." If you're waiting until you're ready to go, you may never be ready to go. At least part of the preparation is proceeding to work on what you're trying to get ready to do.

Are you procrastinating and delaying action on what God wants you to do? What excuse have you come up with that sounds logical? Are you ready to face the truth of why you are delaying? I hope that you are, for God knew your weakness when He first spoke to you. Despite that, He is holding out a chance for you to fulfill your purpose. Are you ready to stop delaying and begin acting? Today could be the day when you finally stop asking questions, trying to figure it all out. For your sake, I hope it is.

STUDY #47
MOSES: "WHAT IF I FAIL?"

Let's continue our studies on Moses and his comments during his encounter with the Lord at the burning bush. Now it's time to look at his fourth comment: "What if they do not believe me or listen to me and say, 'The Lord did not appear to you'?" (Exodus 4:1) Moses was asking, "What if I fail? What if I'm obedient, but the people are not?" From my own life and experience as a purpose coach, I'm ready to declare that fear of failure is the primary stumbling block for people trying to be more purposeful and productive. You can be so afraid to do the wrong thing that you do nothing, missing opportunities that could be significant.

Are you afraid of failure? Is that what stands between you and your attempt to fulfill your purpose or achieve your goal? Let's look at a famous quote from American president, Teddy Roosevelt, which addressed the issue of failure:

> It is not the critic who counts; not the man who points out how the strong man stumbles, or where the doer of deeds could have done them better. The credit belongs to the man who is actually in the arena, whose face is marred by dust and sweat and blood; who strives valiantly; who errs, and comes up short again and again, because there is no effort without error and shortcoming;

but who does actually strive to do the deeds; who knows the great enthusiasms, the great devotions; who spends himself in a worthy cause; who at the best knows in the end the triumph of high achievement, and who at the worse, if he fails, at least fails while daring greatly, so that his place shall never be with those cold and timid souls who know neither victory nor defeat.

I'm of the opinion that it's better to fail trying to do something than succeed at doing nothing, for the latter isn't really success at all. I've been too concerned in the past with what other people thought. I've also been too concerned with trying *not* to fail instead of trying to succeed.

Are you ready to face your fear of failure? There's only one way to do that, and that's to do something about what you've always said you would do one day. I'm writing to tell you that the "one day" is here and now. I've quoted James 2:17 many times to many people: "In the same way, faith by itself, if it is not accompanied by action, is dead." Take some immediate action that will help you overcome your fear of failure and do something that could change your world.

STUDY #48
MOSES: "JUST A STAFF"

We continue our study of Moses' comments during his encounter with the burning bush. It's time to look at his fifth comment, which was an answer to a question God asked Moses: "'What is that in your hand?' 'A staff,' he [Moses] replied" (Exodus 4:2). Moses was concerned he would fail because of all the things he didn't have. In his mind, Moses didn't have enough knowledge about God, he lacked the confidence, he was too old, and he wouldn't be able to respond to the peoples' questions. God asked him a simple question: "What do you have?"

When God assigned your purpose, He knew your gifts, strengths, and weaknesses. If God was content with that package, why should they be of concern to you? People regularly tell me reasons why they can't fulfill their purpose or dreams. They tell me that they lack the education, they're too young or too old, they don't have the money, or they aren't gifted enough. Have you ever said any of those things? God isn't asking you for an inventory of things that you don't have; He's more concerned that you allow Him to use you and what you *do* have.

Moses went to Egypt with that staff in obedience to God's command. He fulfilled his purpose with what he had in his hand. You will fulfill your purpose the same way. Moses was honest with God; he told Him what he had. God went on to show him that it was enough. (Read Exodus 4:3-9 on your own.) Will you allow God to prove to you that you do have what it takes to do His will as long as you submit what you have to Him?

You need to move beyond the realm of excuses to the kingdom of obedience, face your fears, and obey God. In the process, you need to surrender what you do have to God's empowering touch so that you will be equipped to fulfill your purpose. Moses only had a staff in his hand, and it was enough. What do you have in your hand that will enable you to do what you were created to do?

STUDY #49
MOSES: EXCUSES, EXCUSES

We've almost completed our study of Moses' comments during his encounter with the burning bush. His sixth comment was: "Moses said to the Lord, 'O Lord, I have never been eloquent, neither in the past nor since you have spoken to your servant. I am slow of speech and tongue'" (Exodus 4:10).

With this sixth comment, Moses moved from honest questioning to procrastination. He was working hard to come up with some excuse, any excuse so that he wouldn't have to go to Egypt. If you look hard enough, you'll always find a reason that could exempt you from fulfilling your purpose. We saw some of them in the previous study. Some more reasons I hear on a regular basis are: "I don't like to speak in front of people; my spouse/pastor/leader/supervisor doesn't feel good about me doing that; I'm not sure it's God's will; I'm waiting on the Lord's timing." I've heard these reasons many times, and God has heard them even more often.

I especially want to address the last excuse: "I'm waiting on the Lord's timing." I heard a leader say one time, "The need that you see is your call." He meant that seeing a need that exists is often the only "call" you are going to receive. When I teach about purpose, I ask what is it that you see that you assume everyone else sees. In most cases, everyone does not see what you see. Seeing it then requires that you do something about it, without over-spiritualizing the process. God, who has given you the ability to see the need, will also equip you to address that need. The Lord responded to Moses:

> The Lord said to him, "Who gave man his mouth? Who makes him deaf or mute? Who gives him sight or makes him blind? Is it not I, the Lord? Now go; I will help you speak and will teach you what to say" (Exodus 4:11-12).

Perhaps God is saying the same thing to you. He may be directing you to "go" and "do." As you go, He will help you speak or do whatever it is that He wants you to do. Stop procrastinating and finding excuses to justify your delay. The good news is that it isn't too late. The God of your purpose is extending another opportunity to do His will. Don't disappoint Him or make Him find someone else. You can do it. What's more, you must do it if you are to be a person of purpose.

STUDY #50
MOSES: INTO THE GAME

Let's begin with a story from the world of sports. Several years ago, a professional basketball game was in the final seconds. The coach called time out and issued a play that he hoped would win the game. When play resumed, however, only four of his players were in the game. The fifth player, who was also the star, refused to go back in because he wasn't slated to take the winning shot. He forced the coach to put someone else in although his team won anyway. Players, writers and fans criticized that player for his selfish behavior.

As we look at Moses' seventh comment, we see that Moses, having exhausted all the excuses and questions he could think of, simply refused to go to Egypt. "But Moses said, 'O Lord, please send someone else to do it'" (Exodus 4:13). In essence, Moses said "no" to God! Moses refused to go into the game just like that basketball player. And what was God's response? "Then the Lord's anger burned against Moses" (Exodus 4:14). I hope I never make God angry, but this story proves that it can happen. God is patient but there are limitations to His patience, and we're never quite sure when we will reach them.

People ask me all the time, "Can you refuse your purpose?" and my answer is always, "Yes!" Consider these two passages as examples: "But the Pharisees and experts in the law rejected God's purpose for themselves" (Luke 7:30); and "As God's fellow workers we urge you not to receive God's grace in vain" (2 Corinthians 6:1-2).

You can receive the grace of God's purpose in vain, choosing to ignore or do nothing with it. You can sit on your gifts, choosing to remain in the comfort zone of life rather than experiencing the discomfort of new faith experiences. You can be so afraid of doing the wrong thing that you choose to do nothing instead.

God had answered and addressed each of Moses' questions and concerns so that the real reason for Moses' reluctance could be revealed: Moses just didn't want to do it. Like that star basketball player, Moses just didn't want to go into the game.

How about you? Are you testing God's patience through delay and excuses? The good news is that after Moses said this, God assigned Aaron to go with Moses and then sent them both on their way to Egypt. If you confess that you don't want to fulfill your purpose, and that you're scared, lazy, or lack confidence, then the Lord will still help you! You're not alone in your search for purpose; God is with you, even in your hesitancy. All you must do is acknowledge where you are and ask God's help. He will do the rest. It's time to face reality and move on to do great things for God, just as Moses did. God wants you in the game. Will you go?

STUDY #51
CELEBRATE A FAILURE

I have an idea for an international holiday that we could call "Celebrate a Failure Day." Surprised? Since failure is a common experience among all people, then it must serve some purpose in our lives. I think it comes to teach and train us, to prepare us for the ultimate success that will come if we don't give up. Here are ideas I have for this new holiday:

- If you are a pastor, talk about failure and its role in the life of the believer. Make sure you are clear that it is spiritual to fail.

- Spend time talking with your family, and especially your children, about failure. You may want to focus on one failure in your own life and what you learned from it. This will free your children from the false sense that failure is to be avoided at all costs. Maybe you can have a family failure party! Make sure you laugh a lot, even at yourself.

- If you are in a small group setting, spend some time talking about your failures, how you view failure, and whether you are afraid of failure now.

- In your business, talk about your recent

failures and what you have learned from them. See if these failures have caused co-workers to avoid failure, thus limiting the ability of your business to experiment and grow.

Why am I proposing this unusual action? One business leader said, "Make as many mistakes as you can as quickly as possible. In that way, you'll learn and stay ahead of your competition." When Thomas Watson, founder of IBM, was informed that one of his subordinates had just made a million-dollar mistake, he was asked whether he would terminate that employee. Watson replied, "Heavens no! I just invested $1 million in his education."

As I study the books of Acts, I've noticed that Paul preached one of his greatest sermons in Athens (see Acts 17:15-34), yet he saw very few results. Many feel he went on from there to Corinth a discouraged man. It was in Corinth he experienced tremendous results and even had a visitation from the Lord, who told him, "Do not be afraid any longer, but go on speaking and do not be silent" (Acts 18:9, NAS).

It occurred to me that the Lord often "appeared" to Paul when he was at his lowest and needed encouragement. It was because Paul attempted to do so much that he encountered so much failure and probable depression. It was at those points when God Himself undertook to encourage His man.

Perhaps you are discouraged, or depressed, over a failure. If so, you're ripe for a visitation from God; He's not far from the downhearted, and you qualify. Why not expect a miracle that will encourage your heart and help you overcome your fear or sense of failure? Maybe you can encourage someone else who is struggling with their own sense of humanity and failure.

We must move beyond our ability to tolerate failure

to a place where we can celebrate it by talking about it and learning from it. So don't wait for the holiday to be officially proclaimed. Start celebrating failure today and move through failure to a more meaningful, successful life and career.

STUDY #52
HIT IT HARD
AND WISH IT WELL

Years ago, when I lived in the southern United States, I played a lot of softball. Softball is a game like American baseball, but the ball is bigger, and the pitcher throws it more slowly and underhand. I wasn't a good player, nor was my team very successful. There was one team that was very good, and they defeated our teams most of the time, year after year. They didn't look as sharp as we did because we got new uniforms almost every year. We practiced weekly, yet we never saw them on the practice field. They just knew how to win.

One night we met with some of their players to interview them and see if we could gain the secret of their success. We asked many questions, but then our coach asked their best hitter, "When you're at bat, do you have an offensive philosophy? Do you try to hit it over the fence, or do you try to advance the runners one base at a time?" The man gave our coach a surprised look and announced, "We don't have any philosophy. We just hit it hard and wish it well."

As you seek to fulfill your purpose and be productive, this may be a good strategy to follow. You may just need to "hit it hard and wish it well." In softball, sometimes you can do everything just right and not get to first base. Other times you can do things wrong, but the ball falls in the right spot and you can win the game. Maybe you're waiting for perfection before you try something, or you're frustrated that you've done everything correctly, but things haven't work out. This week you need to overcome your hesitancy or discouragement and go to bat one more time.

This "hit it hard and wish it well" is a principle found in the Bible. The writer of Ecclesiastes wrote about it thousands of years ago:

> If clouds are full of water, they pour rain upon the earth. Whether a tree falls to the south or to the north, in the place where it falls, there will it lie. Whoever watches the wind will not plant; whoever looks at the clouds will not reap. As you do not know the path of the wind, or how the body is formed in a mother's womb, so you cannot understand the work of God, the Maker of all things. Sow your seed in the morning, and at evening let not your hands be idle, for you do not know which will succeed, whether this or that, or whether both will do equally well (Ecclesiastes 11:3-6).

Recently I spent some time improving *The Seven Steps of a PurposeQuest* seminar that I teach. My point is that I did something and now I'm going back to make it better. I conduct a seminar and "hit it hard and wish it well." Now I want you to take some dream, project, or idea, and do the same. You may strike out, but you may also hit a home run. I hope that the coming days bring you closer to the fulfillment of what is in your heart to do or be. Hit it hard and wish it well!

END NOTES

[1]Robert K. Greenleaf, *Seeker and Servant: Reflections on Religious Leadership* (San Francisco: Jossey-Bass Publishers, 1996), p 104.

[2] Richard Leider and David A. Shapiro, *Whistle While You Work* (San Francisco: Berrett-Koehler Publishers, 2001), page 35.

[3] *Ibid.,* page 35.

[4] Laurence Boldt, *How to Find the Work You Love* (New York: Penguin Books, 1996), page 1.

[5] *Ibid.,* page 20.

[6] Henri Nouwen, *Making All Things New* (San Francisco: Harper San Francisco, 1981), page 67.

[7] Brian Mahan, *Forgetting Ourselves on Purpose* (San Francisco: Jossey-Bass, 2002), page 33.

[8] Julia Cameron, *The Artist's Way: A Spiritual Path to Higher Creativity* (New York: J. P. Tarcher, 2002), page 17.

[9] Abraham Maslow, *The Farther Reaches of Human Nature* (New York: Peter Smith Publishers, 1983), page 34.

[10] Os Guinness, *Entrepreneurs of Life: Faith and the Venture of Purposeful Living* (Colorado Springs: Navpress, 2001), page 190.

[11] *Christian History Magazine*, Issue 2: John Wesley, page 34.

[12] Simon Kistemaker, *The Parables: Understanding the Stories That Jesus Told* (Grand Rapids: Baker Books, 1980), pages 124-125.

UNLOCKING THE POWER OF YOU

STUDY #1
THE FIVE REGRETS OF THE DYING

A few years ago, I ran across an article written by an Australian writer, Bronnie Ware, who had devoted many hours to working with patients who are dying. Here is a summary of her journey that led up to her writing the essay:

> After too many years of unfulfilling work, Bronnie Ware began searching for a job with heart. Despite having no formal qualifications or experience, she found herself working in palliative care. Over the years she spent tending to the needs of those who were dying, Bronnie's life was transformed. Later, she wrote an Internet blog about the most common regrets expressed to her by the people she had cared for. The article, also called "The Top Five Regrets of the Dying", gained so much momentum that it was read by more than three million people around the globe in its first year.

In this chapter, I want to summarize the five points from Bronnie's article and then focus on one aspect.

THE FIVE REGRETS

Here are the five regrets that Bronnie discovered in working with those patients close to death over the years:

1. I wish I'd had the courage to live a life true to myself, not the life others expected of me.
2. I wish I didn't work so hard.
3. I wish I'd had the courage to express my feelings.
4. I wish I had stayed in touch with my friends.
5. I wish that I had let myself be happier.

Here is what Ware had to say about the first point, the courage to be true to self and not others:

> This was the most common regret of all. When people realize that their life is almost over and look back clearly on it, it is easy to see how many dreams have gone unfulfilled. Most people have had not honored even a half of their dreams and had to die knowing that it was due to choices they had made, or not made. It is very important to try and honor at least some of your dreams along the way. From the moment that you lose your health, it is too late. Health brings a freedom very few realize, until they no longer have it.

DON'T LET IT BE YOUR REGRET

It takes courage to be true to yourself and who God created you to be. When David went out to fight Goliath, King Saul tried to have David wear his (Saul's) battle armor. Saul was a tall man, however, and the armor didn't fit. David did not try to please the king. Instead, he rejected the armor and took along his sling shot, something that was true to who he was. His success of course is legendary (see 1 Samuel 17:38-40).

Are you wearing someone else's armor? If you are, then you are headed for the number one regret expressed by the dying according to Bronnie Ware's research. I cannot say what you should do, but I can urge you to follow your heart and stop living your life for someone else, unless it is for the Lord. I was challenged by this list, and I hope you are, too. Now that you have read it, it's time to get about the work of living before it's too late.

STUDY #2
WHAT TO DO WITH YOUR BIG HEAD

How do you react when you do something well? What's more, how do you handle it when someone compliments you for something they admire about you? If you're like some, you may not know what to do in those situations. You don't want to appear proud or egocentric, so you may try to minimize your strengths and achievements in your eyes and in the eyes of others. This may seem spiritual or noble, but it's detrimental to your ongoing development and growth.

What should you do when you succeed or receive a compliment? I'm glad you asked. For the answer, however, you must read on.

A BIG HEAD

When David got ready to face Goliath, he made specific and graphic declarations of what he was about to do to Goliath (see 1 Samuel 17). David made good on his promises, killing Goliath with one stone from his slingshot. It's what he did next that answers the questions I raised above.

David cut off Goliath's head! That was one big head not only to cut off but also to carry around. The armies of Israel were encouraged by David's victory, and went forth to win a great victory over the Philistine army. That was one byproduct of David's success. Then David did something else that would be quite uncharacteristic for most of us: "David took the Philistine's head and brought it to Jerusalem, and he put the Philistine's weapons in his own tent" (1 Samuel 17:54).

What did David do with the head? I doubt if he kept it in his tent or made a keychain out of it. He did what most champions did with such spoils of battle. David probably impaled Goliath's head on a post for everyone to see. David celebrated his victory and advertised his achievement! What's more, he kept a souvenir of the battle by keeping the giant's sword in his trophy case.

How does that answer the question of what to do when you achieve success? How does this give you insight into how you should respond when you receive a compliment?

DON'T WORRY THAT A BIG HEAD WILL GIVE YOU A BIG HEAD

David wanted people to see Goliath's head so they would be encouraged to fight their own battles. As any good leader, David wanted the people to see that they didn't have to cower in fear. More importantly, David didn't minimize his success. He didn't say, "Well, it was nothing. You know, it was a lucky shot and God really did it, it wasn't me. You could have done the same thing." Instead, David said, "Look what I've done. What can you do? If this is what God helped me do, what will He help you do?" That's what you need to do as well. If someone compliments you for something you've done or something you are, respond by saying, "Thank you, and I thank God for His help." Don't push their praise away but allow them to admire you and learn from your example.

If you have done something and no one compliments you, then compliment yourself! Admire what you've done. Savor the moment, without being self-conscious or worrying about what others would think of you, or that God is displeased. If you achieve a goal for which you have worked hard, throw yourself a party and invite your friends to celebrate with you. Go out to dinner or take a trip in honor God for your promotion, earned degree or completed project.

David knew how to celebrate his victories and use them to spur himself and others on to greater things. You and I need to do the same. Don't worry about a big head; there will be enough tough knocks and challenges to keep your feet firmly planted.

Thinking like this will help you see that you are not afraid of failure, but afraid of success—of what you will do when you succeed! Can you handle success and the admiration of others? I hope you will learn to broadcast your victories rather than hide behind mediocrity so that no one is offended, and you aren't uncomfortable. Aim for great things, do them and tell the world when you succeed.

STUDY #3
YOUR STRENGTHS AND WEAKNESSES

I am a proponent of functioning in your strengths rather than trying to build up your weaknesses. It makes sense to me that God gives you gifts and talents, which are your strength, and He want you to exercise them as often as possible for the good of others. If you don't have the strength of singing, for example, you don't want to go solo in front of your congregation. This is an easy-to-comprehend example, yet I still find people reluctant to talk about or develop their strengths, especially considering what Paul wrote about functioning in weakness:

> Three times I pleaded with the Lord to take it away from me. But he said to me, "My grace is sufficient for you, for my power is made perfect in *weakness.*" Therefore, I will boast all the more gladly about my *weaknesses,* so that Christ's power may rest on me. That is why, for Christ's sake, I delight in *weaknesses,* in insults, in hardships, in persecutions, in difficulties. For when I am *weak,* then I am strong (2 Corinthians 12:8-10, emphasis added).

How can we resolve these words about weakness with my admonition to function in your strengths? Until

I hosted a recent purpose seminar, I did not know how to resolve it.

During the seminar, we determined that purpose is the answer to your important "*what*" question—*what* should I do with my life? Those in attendance saw that we often derail our consideration of the *what* by thinking about the *how* question—*how* can I possibly support myself and my family by doing this? *how* will it all work out? *how* can I possibly do this at my age (young or old)?

I wrote *what* and *how* on a white board when one of the young ladies in the seminar offered this perspective: "It seems that the *what* is your strength, but the *how* is your weakness. We must accept the *what* but then trust the Lord for the *how*." And I thought, "That's it!"

Look back at what Paul wrote in 2 Corinthians. His weakness was the *how* of his purpose to the Gentiles. He encountered persecution, difficulties and the insults from many—he was clear on the *what* he was given to do, but the *how* was his challenge. He faced opposition on every front and even had to face his own physical limitations that limited his energy. It was in his *how* weakness that the Lord was exalted as He empowered Paul to fulfill his purpose.

Paul saw that he was in his best position for success when he functioned in his purpose, while also facing his limitations and trusting the Lord to somehow make a way. God always did make a way, even when he was in prison or on a sinking ship. When the ship to Rome was going down, Paul was fulfilling his purpose of taking the gospel to the Gentiles as he preached and witnessed to the ship's Gentile crew.

This understanding is important for your PurposeQuest. If you are going to face life's difficulties, you need your purpose strength. At the same time, you will face your own inadequacies and the problems of life that will make your purpose seem like a dream. You will ask the Lord for help with the how, for that is your point of weakness. When He sends help, you will say, like Paul, that you glory in your weaknesses while you function in your strengths.

STUDY #4
THE PARABLE OF
THE PENCIL

A radio guest introduced me to the Parable of the Pencil, and now I am going to introduce, or re-introduce it to you. The Pencil Maker took the pencil aside just before putting him into the box. "There are five things you need to know," he told the pencil, "Before I send you out into the world. Always remember them and never forget, and you will become the best pencil you can be:

1. You will be able to do many great things, but only if you allow yourself to be held in someone's hand.

2. You will experience a painful sharpening from time to time, but you'll need it to become a better pencil.

3. You will be able to correct any mistakes you might make.

4. The most important part of you will always be what's inside.

5. On every surface you are used on, you must leave your mark. No matter what the condition, you must continue to write."

The pencil understood and promised to remember

and went into the box with purpose in its heart. Now replacing the place of the pencil with you, always remember those five points, and you will become the best person you can be.

1. You will be able to do many great things, but only if you allow yourself to be held in God's hand and allow other human beings to access you for the many gifts you possess.

2. You will experience a painful sharpening from time to time by going through various problems, but you'll need it to become a stronger person.

3. You will be able to correct any mistakes you might make.

4. The most important part of you will always be what's on the inside.

5. On every surface you walk through, you must leave your mark. No matter what the situation, you must continue to do your duties. By understanding and remembering, proceed with your life on this earth, having a meaningful purpose in your heart.

Today's question: What lessons can you take away from the Parable of the Pencil?

STUDY #5
WHAT-MAKES-YOU-TICK LIST

It is said that Beethoven at one point stopped writing for his generation, for most ignored, criticized or simply did not understand his music and what he was trying to do. He never stopped writing, however, but rather wrote for future audiences rather than his contemporaries. That is in some sense what I feel I am doing, especially with my book *Changing the Way We Do Church*. I consider that book one of my best. Most of the church doesn't get what I am writing, however, or if they do, it has had little effect as far as I can tell. I'm not whining, and I'm open to the fact that maybe what I have to say isn't as good or relevant as I think it is. The other option is that it is for another time.

A colleague once posed a question in a staff devotion, and it gave me pause. The question was, "What makes you tick?" The answer to that question for Beethoven was to write cutting-edge music that had never been written before. One of the things that makes me tick is to see purpose impact people's lives, and then see that impact make a difference in the life of the local church. As I continued to answer my colleague's question, here's what I came up with:

1. Leadership development
2. Teaching/seminars/speaking
3. Writing

4. Broadcasting and publishing
5. Coaching—making room for others to do their thing
6. Travel anywhere
7. Airports
8. Africa
9. Diversity involvement—working with people who don't look like me
10. Doing new things and creating order from their chaos
11. Reading/study/learning
12. Live events like plays and baseball games
13. Color—for example, I carry two bright orange pens with me everywhere I go

I wrote those things out in about five minutes. I then turned to two of my other colleagues and asked, "What makes you tick?" Neither one had a good answer if they had an answer at all. Now I will ask you: What makes you tick? Take five minutes and write down all the answers you can think of. Then carry that list with you for the next week and add to it as you encounter something else that makes you tick.

Your answers to that question are important, for you will end up doing what makes others tick if you don't face what motivates you. Once you have the list, don't do anything with it just yet. Simply study it and make sure it's complete. In the next chapter, we will create another list to help you understand what stops your clock.

STUDY #6
WHAT-STOPS-YOUR-CLOCK LIST

In the last chapter, I shared a list of things that make me tick. I hope you did the exercise I recommended to generate your own list. Now I want to share the "what stops my clock" list of those things that do not make me tick. It's just as important to identify what is on this list, for while the tick list can energize you, the what-stops-your-clock list will steal your energy and creativity like a bandit and never give any of it back. Here is my list. What's yours?

- Bureaucracy
- Authoritarian, arrogant leadership
- Traditions that don't make sense but carry the weight of law
- Hospital visitation
- Boring meetings
- Boring meetings that I must attend but can't help make them interesting
- People who don't ask me how I'm doing after I ask them
- Stingy people
- Lack of progress on a project

- Nepotism where the family member is not qualified for the position
- Bureaucracy (Oh, I already used that one, but it should count twice because I hate it so much)
- A class taught by a bad or poorly prepared teacher
- Losing a game
- Self-absorbed leadership

As I study that list, I realize that most of those things involve people in one way or another, and some of them involve poor leadership. This shows me that I must be careful when I work with people, because they can take away my energy when they interfere with the task at hand. This list also shows me what my values are. If the things on my list demotivate me, then I must labor to make sure I am not guilty de-motivating others through the same behaviors or traits.

There you have my stop-my-clock list. Now, take five minutes and create yours. Don't spend a lot of time agonizing over it, but once you have it, study it to see what it reveals to you. Are you willing to build your life around the things that make you tick and minimize your encounters with the bandits? I hope you are.

Now that you have your two lists, study them both and see where you investing your time and effort—on things that make time fly or that cause it to drag on in boredom? As things emerge from your lists, begin to change engage activities that are more in line with who you are and what's most important to you.

STUDY #7
ASK YOURSELF 100 QUESTIONS

You may not know your purpose because you don't ask enough good questions. If you are asking the right questions, you may not hold on to your unanswered questions until you find the answers, abandoning the quest. Finding and fulfilling your purpose can be hard work. There are few shortcuts and no easy or pat answers. Even when you discover purpose, it's often difficult to know how and where to invest yourself. In short, a PurposeQuest sometimes involves more heart and effort than a person is willing or able to give, and that may include you.

A well-known motivational speaker has stated that quality questions lead to a quality life. That pertains to your purpose, for you must proactively seek the truth concerning who you are, and part of that seeking is asking the right questions. My job, as a purpose coach and writer, is to equip you with those quality questions. After that, I have faith that the quality answers will come.

Let's look at an example of quality questions from the life of Nehemiah. Nehemiah was interested in Jerusalem and its residents, even though he had never been there. One day a group of travelers caught his attention as they discussed Jerusalem, and he asked them some questions. Their answers provoked him to prayer, thought and action. The rest is history as he found his purpose to go to Jerusalem and rebuild the ruined city. His mission started with good questions.

IOO QUESTIONS

Once I was talking with my sister-in-law and the issue of asking good questions came up. She said those questions reminded her of a recommended exercise in a book I had given her by Michael Gelb entitled *How to Think Like Leonardo da Vinci.* Here is a recommendation that Gelb made:

> In your notebook, make a list of a hundred questions that are important to you. Your list can include any kind of question if it's something you deem significant: anything from "How can I save more money?" or "How can I have more fun?" to "What is the meaning and purpose of my existence?" and "How can I best serve the Creator?"
>
> Do the entire list in one sitting. Write quickly; don't worry about spelling, grammar, or repeating the same question in different words (recurring questions will alert you to emerging themes). Why a hundred questions? The first twenty or so will be "off the top of your head." In the next thirty or forty, themes often begin to emerge. And, in the latter part of the second half of the list, you are likely to discover unexpected but profound material.
>
> When you have finished, read through your list and highlight the themes that emerge. Consider the emerging themes without judging them. Are most of your questions about relationships? Business? Fun? Money? The meaning of life?[1]

I came up with my hundred questions in about 30

minutes, so it doesn't take long. It was a valuable exercise that I have been processing for quite some time. Why not invest 30 minutes in your own questions that will help you discover your purpose. Then pick out a few questions and pursue them until you get an answer.

STUDY #8
STRIKE THE WATERS

I have enjoyed my role as a college professor, and hope to do more and more teaching as the years go on. I love teaching new classes I have never taught before, because they direct me into areas of study that I would not ordinarily pursue. That causes me to grow. I recently completed my certification to conduct online classes, which is the wave of the future.

In a sense, I have been preparing for those classes all my life. I have diligently followed an aggressive reading and listening program for decades. I went back to school at age 57 to earn a Doctor of Ministry degree, and I have attended many seminars and certification classes. While I must prepare for each course, I am ready to teach because of my years of preparation. It makes me think of Elisha, who had traveled with Elijah and served him for many years. When Elijah was taken, Elisha took up the cloak Elijah had left behind and did what he had seen Elijah do:

> Elisha then picked up Elijah's cloak that had fallen from him and went back and stood on the bank of the Jordan. He took the cloak that had fallen from Elijah and struck the water with it. 'Where now is the Lord, the God of Elijah?' he asked. When he struck the water, it divided to the right and to the left, and he crossed over (2 Kings 2:13-14).

When I teach, I am striking the waters and, much to my ongoing amazement and joy, they part. God is helping me, even when I have not prepared as I desired for certain weeks. When that happens, a lifetime of preparation comes forth, and God does the rest—to God be the glory.

PERFECTIONISM

All this has delivered me from a desire for unrealistic perfectionism. I still pursue excellence, but I no longer define excellence as an absence of mistakes. I define it as a heart attitude that I will do my best with what I have and who I am and trust the Lord for the rest. When I began my online Bible studies, I forced myself to send them out every week without proofing them. This made me uncomfortable, but I wanted to put the emphasis on creating the studies and not perfecting the studies.

Years later when I went back to edit those studies, I found the mistakes. In the nine years that I sent out those weekly studies, I never got an email or a comment drawing attention to the mistakes. Almost every week, however, I received emails of gratitude and appreciation for sending the studies. People shared what the studies meant to them, and I realized that my pursuit of perfection could have cost those people the help they received if I had not sent the studies out until they were "ready."

What about you? What are you preparing to do for the Lord that may take a few years or decades to complete? More importantly, when will you be ready to strike the waters like Elisha did and see the same results you watched others produce? Have you allowed your pursuit of perfection to prevent you from producing something that could honor God and help others?

Now may be the time for you to do what you have been talking about and preparing to do. Why not find a good situation to test the waters and see if God will act on your behalf because you have prepared for Him to do so?

Don't put it off any longer. If you are not ready (and you may be more ready than you think you are), however, I urge you to get ready. Today I thank God I prepared for this day by His direction and grace, and I am having a wonderful time. God wants you to have the same experience. If I can help, let me know.

STUDY #9
DISTURB ME

During a recent seminar, I read a prayer I found in a book entitled *Chazown: A Different Way to See Your Life* by Craig Groeschel. I urge you to pray this prayer included below, if you dare. I already did and it works, but not in the way you may think.

DISTURB ME

The prayer was first prayed by Sir Francis Drake, who sailed around the world for England in 1577. The prayer goes like this:

> Disturb us, Lord, when we are too well pleased with ourselves, when our dreams have come true because we have dreamed too little, when we arrive safely because we have sailed too close to the shore.

> Disturb us, Lord, when with the abundance of things we possess, we have lost our thirst for the waters of life; having fallen in love with life, we have ceased to dream of eternity; and in our efforts to build a new earth, we have allowed our vision of the new Heaven to dim.

> Disturb us, Lord, to dare more boldly, to venture on wider seas where storms will show your

mastery; where losing sight of land, we shall find the stars. We ask you to push back the horizons of our hopes; and to push into the future in strength, courage, hope, and love.[2]

Now you see why I cautioned you about this dangerous prayer. As I travel and talk with people, however, it is a prayer that many desperately need to pray, and you may be among them.

SHRINKING BACK

Look at this passage found in Hebrews 10:35-39 that address the issues raised in the *Disturb Us* prayer:

> So do not throw away your confidence; it will be richly rewarded. You need to persevere so that when you have done the will of God, you will receive what he has promised. For in just a very little while, 'He who is coming will come and not delay. But my righteous one will live by faith. And if he shrinks back, I will not be pleased with him.' But we are not of those who shrink back and are destroyed, but of those who believe and are saved.

You may respond that you are living by faith, but perhaps that is because you are living so small. Your goals are timid, and your vision tiny because your fears have overwhelmed you. You are not doing anything beyond what you can see right in front of you, and to some it appears that you are living a busy life. Instead, you are living woefully below what God has for you. You have shrunk back to your comfort zone but describe it as only a place of respite, dreaming of what you will do one day when the conditions are just right.

I hope the previous paragraph doesn't describe your life. If it does, however, and you know it, now is the time to do something about it by setting some goals and living by faith once again. The beauty of doing this is that you don't need any idea of how you will accomplish those dreams; that's where the faith comes in. If you've decided, however, that faith is just too demanding or stressful, then you may be guilty of shrinking back, thus incurring God's displeasure.

Your choice is clear: have faith and please God or shrink back and displease God. I hope you will choose wisely between the two. If you choose faith, then go back to the beginning of this chapter and pray the *Disturb Us* prayer every day this week. As you do, God will answer and will certainly disturb you with new visions and dreams before very long. Then you can set sail for destinations unknown, enjoying the journey as you venture onward in life.

STUDY #10
ECONOMIC TERRORISM

When you set out to fulfill your purpose, something interesting happens, you will be tested as to whether you can maintain purpose. Often this test is financial and involved what I refer to as financial terrorism. If the enemy of your soul can't keep you from purpose, he will try to surround your "city" and starve you into surrender, hoping you will give up and go back to your old job, your old way of life, your place of comfort. What's even more interesting is that God allows this to happen, for those tough times will equip you for your future success and keep you humble. This economic terrorism is a million-dollar experience that you would not give ten cents to go through again.

But you may ask if is there any biblical precedent for this terrorism. I believe there is. To see if you agree with me, you will have to read on.

THE LAND

God brought Abraham out of his homeland and promised to give him the land to which God was sending Him. He also promised that Abraham's descendants would be more numerous than the sands on the seashore. I wonder how Abraham knew about seashore sand, unless he had visited the beach during his lifetime? Anyway, I digress.

Abraham pursued his purpose and entered the land

God had promised. Yet a curious thing happened, for at one point Abraham had to leave the very land God had given him. Why did he leave? The Bible tells us: "Now there was a famine in the land, and Abram went down to Egypt to live there for a while because the famine was severe" (Genesis 12:10).

God gave Abraham the land but then Abraham had to leave it because there was a famine, and he would have starved! Why would God allow this to happen? One reason is so that God could reveal the work that still needed done in Abraham's' life and faith. This is evident when Abraham decided to misrepresent his wife Sarah, portraying her as his cousin and not his wife. That showed that Abraham's faith in the Lord was not where it needed to be for the ultimate fulfillment of his purpose. The other reason was to teach Abraham to hold on to God's promise and not look at the circumstances surrounding the promise.

Your own lack during your economic terrorism season will also reveal the real you, just like it did in Abraham's case.

MY OWN JOURNEY

I went through my own economic terrorism in 2001. There were days when I didn't think we were going to survive. I thought about turning aside to a job or some other means of support, but I decided to endure and press on. Years later, I am glad I did. What's more, my only regret is that I didn't engage my purpose earlier than 2001!

Today I am stronger and have more faith in God than ever before. I am not intimidated by my lack of resources as I set my goals. Famine, survival and economic terrorism taught me a lot about myself and God. I am a better servant of God today not only because of purpose, but because of my lack when I started to move forward.

Are you experiencing economic terrorism of some sort? This isn't an indication you have done something wrong, but something right! Don't panic, but instead, trust God. You will live, although there will be times when are you are convinced you won't! When it's over, you will see what God was doing and has done, and you will rejoice. During the famine, it's difficult to do that.

If you are going through economic terrorism, use this time to strengthen your faith and keep your eyes on God. He is in control and won't allow your lack to last one day longer than it must. It must take place, however, and its end will bring not only a sigh of relief but also the great blessing that God had in mind as the result all along.

STUDY #11
TIME OUT, TIME OFF

I have been a college instructor since 1998. I enjoy being assigned classes to help fill out the semester course schedule because they help direct my study and help me grow. One semester I was asked to teach "The Theology of Paul from Romans to Timothy." While preparing for this class, I saw something about Paul I had never noticed.

TIME OUT

When Paul was at the peak of his ministry, he felt led to go to Jerusalem:

> "And now, compelled by the Spirit, I am going to Jerusalem, not knowing what will happen to me there. I only know that in every city the Holy Spirit warns me that prison and hardships are facing me. However, I consider my life worth nothing to me; my only aim is to finish the race and complete the task the Lord Jesus has given me—the task of testifying to the good news of God's grace" (Acts 20:22-24).

When Paul arrived in Jerusalem, he found that many in the city were ambivalent toward him and his ministry, so he tried to appease them by appearing in the Temple. This led to a near riot during which Paul was seized by the Roman guards to save his life. From there he went to Caesarea to stand trial and eventually appealed to Caesar, which took him to Rome, a place he had desired to visit for some time.

It was a four-year period from the time that Paul arrived in Jerusalem until the end of the book of Acts when he was under house arrest in Rome. And that is the point that made an impression on me. At the time when Paul was most knowledgeable and experienced, when he could have been so productive traveling to strengthen the churches and disciples, God took Paul out of circulation for four years.

TIME OFF

Why would God do this? I am not second guessing the Lord, for He knew what He was doing during this period of Paul's life. Yet let's examine those four years from Paul's perspective. Paul had done so much for so long and then he was forced to take a time out. During those years, his enemies were free to move into the churches he planted to distort Paul's gospel. Paul could do nothing but trust God and the people who had served his ministry to sort out the problems.

It was during these four years that Paul wrote what are known as his prison epistles-Ephesians, Philippians, Colossians and Philemon. To write with the insight Paul had, he needed time to reflect on his message and think. He could not produce fresh material and do what he had been doing as an itinerate preacher. God had him take some time off through a time out, and the results were letters that still impact the world today. Paul had to let go of his today to embrace his tomorrow. Oh yes, and suffering played a big part in this four-year season of personal growth and development.

Maybe that's where you are. If God has used you, He may be giving you time off to sharpen and freshen your perspective. It's not easy to go from busy to full stop, but those seasons help define who you are and the legacy you will leave. Don't fight it, no matter how difficult the time out may be. Instead make the most of your time off from being in charge and busy. In sports, every time out ends with play being resumed, and the same will be true for you.

STUDY #12
SELF-PROMOTION 1

I had an interesting chat on Facebook with a friend who was in turmoil. He is talented and gifted but struggles when it comes to what he called "self-promotion." He asked me how, after a lifetime of being taught that any kind of promoting self is wrong, how he could step forward and talk about himself, his gifts and what God has put in his heart to do?

That's a great question and one that I have pondered for a long time. It has been an interesting dynamic that people are happy that I write books. Those same people are unhappy when I try to sell them, deeming my efforts shameless self-promotion. Why wouldn't I tell people I have a book that can help them with the specific issue that is addressed in the book? In the minds of some, that's just plain wrong.

CONCEIT

The main concern with self-promotion is best summarized in Philippians 2:3, where Paul wrote: "Do nothing out of selfish ambition or vain conceit. Rather, in humility value others above yourselves." Many conclude after reading this verse that talking about yourself in almost any situation is wrong or at least improper, and ambition is in bad taste if not downright evil. Are these interpretations correct?

Here are some thoughts off the top of my head for this discussion:

- When Paul wrote his letters, he clearly identified himself as an apostle.

- David approached Goliath and declared what he was going to do to the giant in no uncertain terms.

- Jesus made many claims, although sometimes veiled to hide from unbelievers, concerning who He was and what He had come to do

Let's examine that last point a little more.

A PUBLIC FIGURE

Jesus' family thought he was self-promoting and eager to be a public figure as you can see from John 7:3-4: "Jesus' brothers said to him, 'Leave Galilee and go to Judea, so that your disciples there may see the works you do. No one who wants to become a public figure acts in secret. Since you are doing these things, show yourself to the world.'" It's comforting to know that Jesus' family thought He was self-promoting. To some extent they were correct. He was promoting, but with a purpose. Is that possible for to do the same?

When you consider it, weren't Jesus' miracles a means by which He could gather a crowd to announce the coming of His kingdom? Did not the Father make Jesus a household name and a celebrity in all of Israel? Did Jesus gather disciples whom He then sent out to extend His work and announce God's plan with even greater fervor and success than He did?

We are not going to settle this issue in this chapter, but I wanted to start the dialogue with these thoughts. What do you think? Is it wrong to promote yourself? When, if ever, is it permissible? Does Philippians 2:3 prohibit any kind of ambition or marketing? I leave you to ponder these questions until you read the next chapter.

STUDY #13
SELF-PROMOTION 2

The issue before us is this: What is self-promotion and is it inappropriate to engage in it? There are some who look with disfavor and even disdain on anyone or any ministry that is involved in what they consider self-promoting activities. Are they correct? Does the Bible forbid self-promotion? Let's continue our discussion of this misunderstood concept.

YOUR LIGHT

My thoughts for this chapter come from Matthew 5:14-16, where it says to do your deeds so others can see:

> "You are the light of the world. A town built on a hill cannot be hidden. Neither do people light a lamp and put it under a bowl. Instead, they put it on its stand, and it gives light to everyone in the house. In the same way, let your light shine before others, that they may see your good deeds and glorify your Father in heaven."

Later in the same sermon, Jesus gave this warning:

> "Be careful not to practice your righteousness in front of others to be seen by them. If you do, you will have no reward from your Father in heaven. So when you give to the needy, do not announce

it with trumpets . . ." (Matthew 6:1-2).

Here we have an important distinction between self-ish and godly self-promotion. On the one hand, we are not to parade our righteous acts, such as giving alms, which will glorify self. On the other hand, we are to do our good deeds in such a way that others will see them and glorify God.

Since God has given you your gifts and purpose that enables you to do your good deeds, then I conclude that, in most cases, it is permissible to let people know what you can do, when God enables and empowers you to do it. For example, I am a gifted event coordinator and administrator. I am also a quick and efficient writer. I sense God helping me when I do those things and the feedback over the years has been positive.

Is it wrong to tell others about those gifts? If they need an event planned or some administrative help, have I sinned if I advertise my abilities so others know that I can effectively serve them in those areas?

SERVICE

What's more, if God has given you gifts and a purpose to be used to help others, then isn't letting people know what you can to serve them consistent with letting your light shine as we read above? 1 Peter 4:10 states, "Each of you should use whatever gift you have received to serve others, as faithful stewards of God's grace in its various forms." When I write a book, am I permitted to tell others that I have written it? Can I set up a book table to sell those books or even to give them away? Is it self-promoting when I honestly feel what I have written can help the reader, and therefore I want them to know that the book exists?

It probably is selfish self-promotion if I tattoo the name of my book to my right hand to make sure everyone sees it. It is selfish if I shift every conversation to a discussion of what I can do. If my self-promotion is solely for the purpose of making money or advancing my career, then I have stepped over the line. If my intent is right, however, and I want to serve others with the gifts God has given me, then it seems that I am not engaging in self-promotion but rather God-promotion.

Paul seemed content with those who were doing good work for the wrong reason. In Philippians he penned this amazing statement:

> It is true that some preach Christ out of envy and rivalry, but others out of goodwill. The latter do so out of love, knowing that I am put here for the defense of the gospel. The former preach Christ out of selfish ambition, not sincerely, supposing that they can stir up trouble for me while I am in chains. But what does it matter? The important thing is that in every way, whether from false motives or true, Christ is preached. And because of this I rejoice (Philippians 1:15-18).

It seems that some people were preaching Christ out of rivalry with other ministries, promoting themselves as they preached the gospel. How did Paul deal with that fact? He rejoiced because he knew God could use those all-too-human motives to accomplish His purposes.

Let's continue our discussion in the next two chapters, for it's important for you to come to grips with when to self-promote and when to fall back.

STUDY #14
SELF-PROMOTION 3

Let's continue our discussion of self-promotion trying to determine what it is and if it permissible under any circumstances for a believer.

MAGNIFY THE LORD

In the Old Testament, we are told to magnify the Lord. We have made that simply a matter of praise and worship where we exalt and describe God's attributes in clear and exuberant musical expressions. Stop and think about that word "magnify." Doesn't it also mean to take the smallest thing and make it larger, so it is easier to see and examine? Could it mean that we are to take the smallest thing that God has done through us and in us and make it *bigger* for all to see, not with the intent to see us, but in seeing us to help others see Him?

Is self-promotion, done with right intent, really any different than giving a testimony? When God does something for you—provides, heals, delivers or reveals—is it wrong to stand up and say what He has done? So if God has given you a gift or purpose, is it any different to broadcast the truth of what God has done in and through you? And when you do, is that not the same as magnifying the Lord—taking His work in you and "blowing it up" for all the world to see.

INTENT

Self-promotion can come from two sources: the selfish desire to promote yourself, or the desire to further God's work through you as you serve others. Consider what Paul said in Romans 11:13-14 (NKJV): "For I speak to you Gentiles; inasmuch as I am an apostle to the Gentiles, I magnify my ministry, if by any means I may provoke to jealousy those who are my flesh and save some of them."

In the NKJV, it states that Paul magnified his office. Other translations of that verse render it "proud of, make as much as I can of, glorify my ministry." Paul magnified his ministry so he could win more Jews to the gospel. Paul promoted what he did because God appointed him, and Paul knew that his work was the most important work in the world. He was not concerned with what others thought, only what God thought. Paul was telling the truth with the right motives, and therefore he magnified himself so he could ultimately magnify the Lord.

Your job is not just to magnify the Lord by behaving and not robbing banks or watching bad movies. Even non-believers do those things. What they cannot do that you can is to express God's love to His creation, specifically through your purpose, gifts and goals. Perhaps it is time you faced the fact that your distaste for what you call self-promotion is really a means to protect yourself from criticism and be-ing misunderstood. Jesus and Paul "promoted" and were criticized; can you expect any different treatment?

STUDY #15
SELF-PROMOTION 4

We have been discussing the delicate and sensitive issue of self-promotion, trying to determine if it is ever appropriate for believers to draw attention to themselves. There are some that oppose this concept under any conditions and then there are others who have no problem "tooting their own horn" every chance they get. Let's wrap up our discussion in this chapter.

THE CHRISTMAS STAR

It seems to me that the star the Magi followed was a publicity gimmick of sorts. It appeared to announce the birth and location of Jesus the Messiah. It seems that the only ones who saw it were some men from the East, and even Matthew is the only gospel writer who tells the star story:

> After Jesus was born in Bethlehem in Judea, during the time of King Herod, Magi from the east came to Jerusalem and asked, "Where is the one who has been born king of the Jews? We saw his star when it rose and have come to worship him" (Matthew 2:1-2).

After they had heard the king, they went on their way, and the star they had seen when it rose went ahead of them until it stopped over the place where the child was. When they saw the star, they were overjoyed. On coming to the house, they saw the child with his mother Mary, and they bowed down and worshiped him. Then they opened their treasures and presented him with gifts of gold, frankincense and myrrh (Matthew 2:9-11).

The star was precise and allowed the men to prepare in advance for their journey by bringing gifts. There were many other events that served to promote the birth of Jesus, but this one is special. All the other events came to people who were passive and not involved in obtaining the promotions—the shepherds were at work when the angels appeared and God sovereignly chose Mary and Joseph (they had not been seeking any role in the Christmas story).

The Magi were different because they were *looking* for the star and then travelled probably hundreds of miles at great personal expense and discomfort to find what the star was promoting. When I pondered this, I saw self-promotion in a whole different light, pardon the pun.

THE SEEKERS

The star came for those who had need, who were diligently searching for that star. Someone had told the Magi that a King would be born, and they and their ancestors had searched to find who He was for centuries. They had faith and they had need, for they came not only to honor the King but also to worship Him. They were hungry for the things of God and God sent a promotional star just for them. Perhaps other saw it, but no one else followed it but these Magi.

You should self-promote not for your benefit but for the benefit of those who are seeking who you are, what you have, and what you can do. If you can pray and people are healed, then healed people need you by the will of the Lord who gave you the gift of healing. If you can write, then you let others know you can, for someone is out there searching for a "star," something to lead them to what they were seeking to find.

If you have died in Christ and belong to Him, then your gift, purpose and role in society are not your choice or call. If God wants to make you a household name, it's none of your business. There are some members of the body who are created to be behind the scenes, but there are some who are made to be seen. Into whichever category you fall, your life is not your own. It belongs to God and others.

Let's get over any vestiges of false humility that say, "If God or anyone needs me, they can come find me. I am not going to help them by self-promoting, for that is not spiritual or proper." If that's how you think, I advise you to "get over it!" and allow all those who need to see your star do that so they know where you live so they can find the help they need that can only come from you. Then they will do just what the Magi did—they will worship *Him*, not you—and that is exactly where your self-promoting activities should lead.

STUDY #16
I LEARNED TO SPEAK BY NOT SPEAKING

It may sound like a paradox when I write that I learned to speak by *not* speaking. After all, isn't the essence of public speaking someone standing in front of a crowd and sharing thoughts or lessons? How can anyone learn how to do something by not doing it? Let's examine those questions more carefully and see if we can come up some answers that make sense.

ELEVEN YEARS

I was an associate pastor for 11 years from 1978 to 1989. While I had many chances to lead a small home group, I only got two chances in those 11 years to speak before the entire church. The second time I spoke was the last Sunday before I left, so it's an accurate statement that I averaged one talk every 11 years. That's a lot of preparation time between messages, don't you think?

What did I do all those 600 Sundays, plus conferences and special meetings, when I watched and listened to countless other speakers? I got ready to speak!

I knew that one day I would address large audiences, even though I was far from doing that during those 11 years. First, I would visualize myself speaking before people. I tell audiences today that I saw them *before* I ever came to be with them. Second, I studied the speakers I witnessed. I watched what worked and what didn't work when they spoke. I fashioned in my mind what kind of speaker I would be before I ever got a chance to speak, just by watching and learning. The most difficult thing during those years was to watch ineffective speakers when I knew in my heart that I could do a better job.

Third, I prepared things to say, even though I had no invitations or speaking engagements at which to say them. I created the *Life is a Goldmine* seminar in 1985, well before I ever had an invitation to deliver it. I prepared the slides, outlines and material. I had a few chances outside of my local church to speak, and I made the most of those opportunities, although at times I wasn't very effective.

Finally, I never gave up my dream, even though I had few opportunities to speak. I watched comediennes, listened and read great speeches of history, and went to school to earn a doctorate. I did all I knew to do. There were times I was so discouraged when nothing happened to advance my vision that I wept with sadness—but I *never* gave up.

THE BREAKTHROUGH

Then I moved to Orlando in 1989 to pastor a church, at which time I also began to speak in jails and prisons. I spoke once a week at the church but often spoke six or seven times a week to men and women behind bars. I went from not speaking to nonstop speaking. Today, I have no lack of speaking engagements, and I continue to hone my skills. My main preparation, however, was during those 11 years of non-activity.

What is the lesson here that is important for you to grasp? It's found in Proverbs 22:29: "Do you see a man skilled in his work? He will serve before kings; he will not serve before obscure men."

I don't care what your dream is. If you spend time

pursuing excellence and becoming good at what you do, you won't have to go looking for "kings." The kings will come looking for you. Don't waste any more time waiting for your breakthrough or trying to make something happen. Instead, invest your time in preparing for the day when your breakthrough comes, and that preparation can begin the minute you finish reading this chapter.

STUDY #17
FIGHTING YOURSELF

You are probably familiar with what Jesus said in John 7:38: "Whoever believes in me, as the Scripture has said, streams of living water will flow from within him." When you believe in Jesus, there is a flow that emanates from you and the water from that flow, while originating in the Spirit, should taste like you. It is comprised of your gifts, personality, the expressions of your life's work, your values, life philosophy and worldview. The flow can't be bitter with anger or unforgiveness, and it can't be salty with lies and deception. It should also not be artificially flavored to taste like someone else's water. Other than that, the water should taste like you.

This is important because you may be among the many who believe that your water is "bad." If it isn't bad, you may think it needs to have another flavor or maybe some fizzy gas added. Many people are fighting themselves, who they are and what they like, even trying to distance themselves from the dreams in their hearts. If that's you, can you recognize how counterproductive it is for you to be opposing yourself?

YOUR FLAVOR

I love live sporting events. I make people laugh. I thrive when I travel and am bored with the mundane. I love teaching, and dread bureaucracy. I love to write and sign books, even shaking hands and posing for a picture or two with my "fans." That is who I am and what my water tastes like. My writing, speaking and consulting has my "flavor," and it flows out of me freely. That water tastes like purpose, productivity, goal setting and being true to yourself. Can you describe to me the flavor of your living water?

Are you filtering the water for impurities and then letting it gush from your life? Or are you damming up the flow, trying not to be who you are? Keep in mind, the water that flows is not for your benefit; it's for others to drink. In this case, it's alright for people to flavor their water to taste like yours, until they can develop their own.

Is there anything you enjoy doing or being that you are trying to curtail or adjust? Maybe those characteristics or interests are part of your flow, and you should stop interfering with their expression. Perhaps a characteristic that you are convinced must change is something God built into you. When you oppose it, you are opposing God, telling Him He made a mistake when He put that in you.

Based on this truth, I will continue to smile and shake hands as I go, not worrying about why I enjoy it as much as I do. I want to be who God made me to be and if anyone has a problem with that, it is their problem and not mine. At one point in my life, I tired of opposing myself and I hope you get tired of opposing yourself, too.

STUDY #18
EXILED

I have taught a course called "Apocalyptic Literature" on several occasions, and it is always a challenge because of the preconceived ideas the students have. I focus the class on John's Revelation but have also looked at apocalyptic sections in Daniel and Ezekiel. One thing that struck me about all those authors is that they were in exile when they received their revelation. John was on Patmos and the other two were in Babylon. I thought it interesting that they were all in foreign lands when they received a coded message from heavenly headquarters revealing important truth. That insight led me to reflect on my own exile and the role it played in my personal development and life message. Let me explain.

EXILED

In 2001, I made a major life and ministry transition. I went from the phone ringing off the hook to no one calling. My calendar, once chock full to overflowing, was empty. People called me *not* to come visit them, but rather to stay away. The only door that was open to me, with a few exceptions, was in Africa. I have always said that God will make His will clear by eliminating all other options. I knew without a doubt Africa was where I was to spend my time.

When I started to travel there, I went for two weeks

at a time. Then I expanded it to four, then eight and then at times up to 14 to 16 weeks. When I add up all the time I spent in Africa from 2001 to 2009, it came to a total of 4.5 years. I refer to that time as my exile.

There were days and nights during my exile where no one knew where I was but the Lord. I wasn't imprisoned during those years, but I was in a place where I was pretty much alone and had lots of time to think, write and reflect. Those years represent a million-dollar experience that I would not give you ten cents to go through again. It was valuable but painful, priceless but costly, and I learned a lot about myself in those years.

Some of what I learned was what I had to unlearn, for there were attitudes and habits that were not appropriate for what the Lord had in store for me in the coming years.

PURPOSE

God had a purpose for my exile, just like He did for John, Daniel and Ezekiel. Sometimes you must have a radical break from your routine for God to reveal Himself to you in new ways. He needs to take you out of your comfort zone to new levels of intimacy and insight, and that can only happen when it's you and Him and very few others. Exile is painful, but it is also critical if you are to reach your full potential.

Like the three apocalyptic authors, I too gained much insight from my exile. I faced and embraced my creativity during my exile. It is when I confronted negative thinking that was limiting God's work in my life. It was also when I learned to trust Him for more than ever before.

God has a purpose for your exile, too. You may find yourself alone or out of the loops that were once an integral part of your life. You haven't done anything wrong, but God must take you away from life as you have known it to speak to you and work on some things. The three exiled authors were all productive in their exile. What's more, they received and wrote about things that still impact the world today. God knew what He was doing with them, He knew what He was doing with me, and He knows what He is doing with you. Trust Him.

Don't only trust Him, however, but make your exile a development time that will serve you well in the coming years. Learn, study, grow, try new things, make new friends but most of all plumb the depths of God's love and purpose for you. When your exile ends, and it almost always ends, you will be a new and better version of your old self, and who knows what revelation you will receive during that time. For while all others may forsake you, God never will, and that is the most important thing to know about exile. Before you had to share your time with others; in exile you have all the time in the world for God. Make the most of it and have faith that your exile will eventually end and you will be able to come "home" once again.

STUDY #19
ANOINTED IGNORANCE

In my career as a college instructor, I have taught 34 different undergraduate classes and nine graduate courses. The usual philosophy is for an instructor to focus on one area or topic, so that the professor can continue to build on his or her expertise. That ensures that the students are getting the best the professors have to offer in their area of interest and emphasis.

Just so you don't misunderstand, I am not teaching physics or astronomy, subjects for which I know nothing about. My course subjects are in the areas of theology, biblical studies, and practical church issues. When I teach classes for the first time, I am forced to learn new things. What's more, I am less of an expert, encouraging the students to learn along with me, and our educational journey is much more rewarding when I can create that atmosphere of learning.

These new courses serve one other purpose in my life: Without them and what they force me to do, all I have is anointed ignorance. Let me explain what that term means.

AN EXAMPLE

If God pours out His Spirit on me (or you), we have some measure of anointing. Yet if I am ignorant (not stupid, just ignorant—capable but undeveloped), then I have

God's anointing, but He doesn't have very much to anoint. Therefore, I have anointed ignorance. I have His Spirit, but I don't have the necessary knowledge or wisdom to go with it.

Here's an example. Perhaps you are talking with someone, and you think of a verse of Scripture that could help them at that point in time. The problem is that you don't have your Bible with you. You have the desire to help, perhaps even the anointing to help, but you don't have the knowledge to help. You have anointed ignorance.

Now let's say that you had taken the time and made the effort to memorize that passage. Now when you are talking to a person and the "anointing" is present, the knowledge is also present and you can share that passage, even though you don't have your Bible.

THERE'S MORE

In addition to all this, recent studies prove that your brain never gets old and wears out. It maintains its ability to learn and develop new habits and thinking patterns all your life, barring some disease or trauma. Therefore, you can keep confronting your areas of ignorance by continuing to learn and grow mentally and intellectually, thus increasing your usefulness to God and His people.

I went back to school later in life than many typically do and I now teach as often as I can because I still have a lot of ignorance. The only way to rectify that is to learn and then offer my learning to God so that He can use it for His purpose and glory. What's more, God does not promote potential; He promotes people who have developed their potential, those who have confronted their ignorance during their anointing.

Are you waiting for God to promote you *before* you have developed yourself and the potential He gave you? Are you asking the Lord to do all He can do while you are not prepared to do all you can do? I urge you to do something to address and develop your potential. Otherwise, you will be stuck with a whole lot of anointed ignorance, which can only be addressed when you take the time and make the effort to fill the void where ignorance resides.

STUDY #20
THE OLD FOLKS WERE RIGHT

When I was younger, I would ask some older folks in church, "How are you doing?" They would sometimes answer, "I got up this morning, so I am fine." I remember thinking, "That's kind of simplistic, and it didn't tell me how they were doing." Now I am in my sixties and have witnessed the burial some of my older and younger friends and peers. When I arise in the morning, I find myself thanking God that He gave me another day. Suddenly what those older folks had to say doesn't sound so strange.

In fact, when I get up these days, I have a litany of things for which I give thanks. I won't go into them here, but with age comes the realization of and appreciation for both what the Lord has done in my life and His gift of another day of life. I meditate on what the psalmist wrote: "Teach us to *number* our days, that we may gain a heart of wisdom" (Psalm 90:12. emphasis added). I don't know how many days I have left, but let's assume I live to be my mother's age of 92. That means I have about 10,000 days left. If I live to be my father's age, I have about 6,000 left. While either option would be nice, for all I know I may only have one day remaining, so I want to make the most of each one of them, whether one or 10,000.

THE QUOTE

Pablo Picasso, the great painter, once said, "Only put

off until tomorrow what you are willing to die having left undone." While I am thankful for today, I want to make the most of it by doing what I can with what I have. I want to run as fast, as far and as long as I can, and if that is a month longer or 30 years, I am already thankful for whatever opportunities the Lord gives me.

When I served as a pastor, I presided over enough funerals to let me know that the old die, and the young can die. No one is getting out of here alive, and all our days are numbered. When I hear people talk about what they will do "one day," I commend them for planning ahead. I also urge them to act with urgency, for that "one day" may be sooner than they think. When I come to the Christmas holiday season, I keep in mind that it could be my last one, so I make the most of it, enjoying every day with those whom I love.

I write with that attitude and I travel to where I want to go now because I am not guaranteed the future. I am grateful for the days I have, and I want to make the most of them. Those older folks taught me to be thankful for every day, recognizing it as the gift that it is—you should do the same. Then once you have started your day with thanks, I want you to aggressively embrace the days you have left—to number them as the psalmist wrote—so you will have a heart of wisdom.

STUDY #21
SUCCCCCESS

My computer spell check is trying to tell me I misspelled succcccess. I spelled it like that on purpose, however, because I want to start a series that focuses on the five c's in succcccess. Since success only has two C's, I thought I would add three more for affect. Each of the five begins with the letter C, thus necessitating the change in spelling.

THE FIRST THREE

Not too long ago I taught a class for a special program of college graduates called "A Love and Theology for the City." In one session, we were discussing with the students what it takes to launch and sustain succcccessful initiatives in poor areas. The more we discussed it, the clearer it was to me that what it takes to succccceed in urban work and ministry is the same as what it takes to be succcccessful in any other area as well. Armed with that conclusion, let's dive into the first three c's.

1. *Curiosity*. If you want to know where to start in your quest for purposeful succcccess, start with your curiosity. Answer the question, "What interests you?" and then pursue the answers. As you do, you may try to "figure out" how you can make money from that interest and, if you can't see how, you will abandon your interests. Don't think like that. Follow your interests and see where they lead you.

God can take some of the simplest interests and help you turn them into a business, organization, movement or project that will bless or edify others.

2. *Creativity*. I have written extensively on creativity, and you can read some of what I have written on my website. Suffice it to say that you were created by the Creator in His image, which is to be creative. There is no end of your ability to be creative as you express your life experience as seen through your eyes. Adam named all the animals in the Garden, and he used his God-given creativity to do so. What assignment has God given you that requires you to do the same?

3. *Competence*. God does not promote people with potential. He promotes those who have developed their potential. You need to become the best you that you can be, and that will require work, training, education, apprenticeship, coaching, spiritual disciplines and godliness. There are no shortcuts to growth and personal development, so don't even look for them. There is only one way to develop yourself and that is to invest time, money and effort into becoming more effective tomorrow than you are today.

THE LAST TWO

Now let's look at the last two c's in succcccess.

4. *Collaboration*. You will need to team and partner with other people if you are going to make a major impact through your life's work. You can't do it all. Rather you must do what you do best and team with others who do what they do best that contributes to the overall effort. What's more, you must know your own strengths and weaknesses and understand how your personality and characteristics will best mesh (or cause some friction) with others.

5. *Commitment*. You will be tested in your resolve to finish the task at hand. God will use your failures and setbacks to conform you to Christ's image. If you faint in the heat of the day, you will not be able to achieve your dreams

or fulfill your purpose. Winston Churchill once addressed an audience of youth, said, "Never, never, never, never, never give up," and then sat down. That's all he had to say, but it was great advice. If you have breath, stay the course.

There you have the five key elements that lead to succcccess. We will take a closer look at each one over the next five chapters and learn how to develop and apply them in your life's work. I have not included any Bible verses in this chapter, but don't worry, there will be plenty in the chapters to come.

STUDY #22
CURIOSITY

In the last chapter, I explained that we are going to be looking at five concepts that all being with the letter C that help spell *succcccess*. I promised to touch on each one of the five in more depth in the coming chapters, so here is the follow up to that promise. I have thought of several more c's since last week, but I am not ready to expand the series, otherwise I will have to spell success "succccccccccccccess." Maybe that would not be such a bad thing, but for now, let's dive into the concept of curiosity and learn how it relates to succcccess.

A BURNING BUSH

We know that Moses tended sheep in the wilderness for forty years! I have been to the Middle East numerous times, and it is a hot place. Moses had to work in this heat year in and year out, and I am sure that every now and then a dry bush would burst into flames due to the super-hot conditions. Then one day Moses saw something unusual that captured his attention:

> Now Moses was tending the flock of Jethro his father-in-law, the priest of Midian, and he led the flock to the far side of the wilderness and came to Horeb, the mountain of God. There the angel of the Lord appeared to him in flames of fire from

within a bush. Moses saw that though the bush
was on fire it did not burn up. So Moses thought,
"I will go over and see this strange sight—why
the bush does not burn up" (Exodus 3:1-3).

What was unusual about this bush is that it burned,
probably a common sight, but the bush was not consumed.
It just kept on burning. Moses could have easily dismissed
this sight and went about his business, but he decided to
investigate further. Upon closer examination, he had a sur-
prising thing happen: "When the Lord saw that he had gone
over to look, God called to him from within the bush, "Moses! Moses!" And Moses said, "Here I am" (Exodus 3:4).

SO WHAT?

Moses did not approach the bush because God called
him. It was his curiosity that caused Moses to pause and
look, and only then did God call out to Moses and initiate
a series of events that changed the course of history. In this
order of events, first came Moses' curiosity, then his reaction, God's call and finally, Moses' response to God. What
does this have to do with your succcccess?

There are many people waiting for God's call.
Perhaps you are one of them. Did you ever consider that
the call may be in what interests you? You are probably busy
and don't see how what interests you can add to your career.
Therefore, you don't pursue what is in your heart. Because
you don't respond to what is in you, you go about your business and wonder why God is not answering your prayers to
be used or promoted.

It was the apostle Paul's interest, his obsession with
persecuting Christians, that led him to be a Christian and
become the Apostle Paul. If God can use Saul's misdirected
interest to direct his steps, then God can use your curiosities
to do the same. Succcccess starts with investigating what
piques your interest. Do something to satisfy your curiosity

this week. Read a book, go to a museum, have lunch with a colleague, or draw a picture.

Don't try to figure out why you are doing it, or what good it will contribute to the long run. Approach it like Moses did the bush or Paul went after the Christians. As you do it, however, listen for God's voice, that may be something as subtle as, "I like this and think I will do it again." That's how you follow your curiosity until it becomes a passion.

STUDY #23
CREATIVITY

In the last chapter, we began a discussion of the five c's in succccccess. If you think succccccess should not be a consideration for you, read these words from Psalm 1:1-3 in the Good News Translation:

> "Happy are those who reject the advice of evil people, who do not follow the example of sinners or join those who have no use for God. Instead, they find joy in obeying the Law of the Lord, and they study it day and night. They are like trees that grow beside a stream, that bear fruit at the right time, and whose leaves do not dry up. *They succeed in everything they do*" (emphasis added).

With that in mind, let's look at the second c in succccess, that being creativity.

YES, YOU ARE!

In 2006, I had a startling revelation and changed my purpose statement from "I *bring* order out of chaos" to "I *create* order out of chaos." It was then that I accepted the fact that I am a creative person, something I had denied up to that point. I began to write and teach about creativity after that, and I have many *articles* on my website devoted to the subject of creativity.

I also have a list of creative expressions sent to me by

my readers over the years after they read some of my material. They listed child raising, letter writing, problem solving, public speaking, and time management as activities people engage in every day that require creativity. This is valuable to understand, because most people consider only artists or poets as creative. If you have children or manage your time, however, you are creative, too!

CREATIVITY FOLLOWS CURIOSITY

In the last chapter, we looked at the first c in succcccess and that is curiosity. Once you are curious and decide to follow your heart and what interests you, it is time to express your creativity. You can then begin to structure your world and invest your time in such a way that your creativity can take shape as a practical expression of who you are. I am interested in writing and have been since I was young. So in 1995 at the age of 45, I started to pursue my interest and today I write every day to an audience all over the world.

I have written 75 books, edited many others, composed more than 1,000 *Monday Memos*, finished a verse-by-verse devotional on the entire New Testament, and wrote a daily devotional online for seven years. Currently I am teaching four college classes and have numerous other creative projects and ideas in the works. I love to do media but got tired of waiting for people to invite me to be part of their media world. Therefore, I started my own online shows and at one time hosted five weekly broadcasts.

You don't have to do any of those things that I am doing to be creative. You simply must be yourself. You cannot be fighting yourself, however, and be creative. My experience is that many people (perhaps even you) are trying to talk themselves out of their creativity instead of into it. With that in mind, I encourage you to read my past *Memos*, think about this in the coming days and embrace your creativity. You cannot be succcccessful without employing your creativity, but you cannot employ it if you deny that it even exists.

It will help you to sit down and in ten minutes list all the creative expressions you have in your life. Once you see and accept that you are creative, your life will change, as mine did, and your creative expressions will leap from your heart and mind into a world that is waiting for them to appear. Have fun and be creative!

STUDY #24
COMPETENCE

In this chapter, let's continue our discussion of the five c's in succcccess with the third c, competence. Let me say at the start that God does not promote or use people with potential. He does not promote holy people simply because they are holy. God promotes and uses holy people who have developed their potential through competence and fruitfulness. Don't believe that? Then read on and see if I can convince you.

PROOF PLEASE

Here are some statements about the importance of competence for you to consider:

1. Daniel. Daniel served with distinction in Babylon. He was promoted because of his gifts that God gave him, but he developed them, as it was said of Daniel: "At this, the administrators and the satraps tried to find grounds for charges against Daniel in his conduct of government affairs, but they were unable to do so. They could find no corruption in him, because he was trustworthy and neither corrupt nor negligent" (Daniel 6:4). Daniel was a great administrator.

2. David. David was a prolific songwriter and poet who honed his skills through regular use. He was also a magnificent warrior and leader, of whom the people sang:

"When the men were returning home after David had killed the Philistine, the women came out from all the towns of Israel to meet King Saul with singing and dancing, with joyful songs and with timbrels and lyres. As they danced, they sang: "Saul has slain his thousands, and David his tens of thousands" (1 Samuel 18:6-7).

3. Esther. Esther was a beautiful woman, by God's design: "This young woman, who was also known as Esther, had a lovely figure and was beautiful" (Esther 2:7b). What did God do with her beauty? He dispatched her to the king's servants, who bestowed beauty treatments on Esther for one year. The result: She was even more beautiful than before!

4. Paul. Paul knew four languages and was from one of the most cross-cultural cities in the Roman Empire. He was a Jew of Jews and a perfect keeper of God's law by his own admission: ". . . as for righteousness based on the law, faultless" (Philippians 3:6). What did God do with this man who had excelled in Judaism? He chose Paul to be His representative to the Gentiles. God took Paul's skill, redirected and perfected it, and used it for His glory.

THE LESSON FOR YOU

The lesson for you should be clear. God uses you to the extent that you have developed your skills and gifts. If you are competent, He will use you. If you are competent and have integrity, He will promote you to the highest levels that your gifts and foundation will allow you to attain. Your succcccess in any field or endeavor is a partnership with God, who provides the grace and opportunities, and you, who develop your competence.

What is your plan for competence? Do you even have one? In what field or effort do you want to be competent, even world-class, in skill and effect? Mind you, I am not suggesting that competence is more important than holiness or integrity. I am saying, however, that without competence your holiness alone will limit God's ability to fully use your potential. Give some thought this week to the importance of competence in succcccess and then go about a one-year, five-year, or lifetime plan to achieve the greatest skill possible for you as you express your purpose and pursue your goals.

STUDY #25
COLLABORATION

We are almost finished with our discussion of the five c's in succcccess. So far, we have covered Curiosity, Creativity, and Competence. In this chapter, let's look at collaboration.

YAY TEAM!

God did not create you with the capability to do everything, just certain things. If you could do it all, you would not have need of anyone else. The same is true for organizations. Even large corporations need to collaborate with others or else build an organization big enough so that everything they need is under one corporate umbrella. In a sense, they are then collaborating within their organization but still must at times build partnerships with other entities.

Here are a few examples of teams working together in the Bible:

1. Joseph and Pharaoh made a great team in Egypt, with Joseph providing the administration and Pharaoh the leadership.

2. Moses and Aaron led the Israelites out of Egypt.

3. Saul and David enjoyed success early in their

partnership as they defeated the Philistines again and again.

4. Nehemiah partnered with the king he served to secure permission and resources to rebuild Jerusalem.

5. Daniel had three friends who served with him in Babylon.

6. Jesus had twelve disciples with whom he collaborated and worked closely.

7. Barnabas and Saul, Paul and Silas, Paul and Luke, and several other combinations worked together to spread the gospel to the Gentiles in the early church.

I hope you are taking in the idea, which is you are going to be succcccessful, you need to collaborate and partner with others, whether you are looking for individual or corporate succcccess.

SOME SUGGESTIONS

Here are some suggestions to enable you to collaborate effectively:

1. *Find those who share your values and ethics.* Don't collaborate with those whom you can't trust.

2. *Partner with your opposite.* This assumes you know your strengths and are willing to collaborate with those who are strong in areas that you aren't.

3. *Know your purpose.* If you know where you are headed, you can join up with people who are on the same road.

4. *Network.* Get out and meet people. Build relationships before you even think of

collaborating. Don't just build a card file of acquaintances but get to know other people and learn what motivates them.

Obviously, this is not an exhaustive teaching on partnerships and collaborations. Instead, it is an exhortation to get out your own little world so you can learn to "play well" with others. If you want to do great things and enjoy succccess, then there is usually no such thing as a one-man or woman act. Successccess usually comes through strategic collaboration.

Stop going it alone and playing it safe and learn to partner with others so that you can enjoy the synergies of joint ventures that will allow you to reach your goals.

STUDY #26
COMMITMENT

The first four traits that begin with the letter C and lead to succcccess are curiosity, creativity, competence and collaboration, which we have discussed in the previous four chapters. Now let's look at the final C word that leads to succcccess, and that word is commitment.

THE WINNER IS

When I think of one standout who had to persevere while being totally committed to God's plan, the winner is Joseph in Genesis. Joseph had his visions from God indicating that he would lead his family when he was only 17 years of age. After that, all hell and parts of heaven broke loose for him and before he knew it, his brothers had sold him into slavery, then covered their deed with their family by concocting a story that Joseph had been devoured by a wild animal.

Joseph initially prospered in Potiphar's Egyptian household and then languished in prison until he was 30 years old. At that time, Pharaoh had his two dreams, and Joseph was summoned to the palace to interpret the dreams. Joseph correctly interpreted that there would be seven bountiful years and then seven of famine. Then he suggested a plan that pleased Pharaoh of how to prepare for those lean years. Pharaoh was pleased, and Joseph went from the dungeon to the palace in a matter of minutes, although he had been a slave in Egypt for 13 years.

It the story ended there, it would be a good one—but it doesn't! Joseph served Egypt during the seven good years, storing up grain and establishing Pharaoh's throne. Then the lean years begin and Joseph's family, not knowing he was alive in Egypt, came down to buy food. They appeared before Joseph and he recognizes them, but they don't recognize him. Joseph eventually told his brothers after he identified who he was, "I will provide for you there, because five years of famine are still to come. Otherwise you and your household and all who belong to you will become destitute" (Genesis 45:11).

What's my point? Joseph was 39 when his brothers came to get food and he revealed himself to them. That means he lived in his dreams before they became reality for 22 years. Can you wait for your dream that long, preparing for the day when it will come to pass?

YOU MAY BE NEXT

If you have done all you can do, are you prepared to wait? Are you committed to whatever it takes to realize succcccess in the long run, whether that is in business, ministry, publishing or some other purpose expression? You can be the next Joseph, if you are willing to pay the price for succcccess as I have spelled out in the last five chapters. Like Joseph, you can have a long wait but then have your life change for the better in five minutes.

As I write, I have yet to realize some of the things I believe God put in my heart. That is why I keep writing, praying, learning and growing. I am committed to do what it takes to see my dreams come true, and that may mean I see them from another vantage point after I am gone to be with Him. Whatever it takes, I won't give up. I invite you to join me in the pursuit of succcccess. Let's not stop until we run as far and fast and as long as we can, as He empowers us.

STUDY #27
HOW HIGH CAN YOU JUMP?

I have a riddle for you: In what two summer Olympic sports is the winner not awarded the gold medal until he or she has failed three times? Then I have a question: Do you know how high you can jump? Let's see if we can answer the riddle and the question, as I explain why I posed them.

THE OLYMPICS OF FAILURE

Do you know the answer to the riddle? The two sports in which you get a gold medal *after* you fail three times are the pole vault and the high jump. The last man or woman left in either competition gets to set the bar at any height, usually just over the world record, and then he or she has three attempts to try and clear that height. Once that person fails to clear three times, the competition is over, and the winner is declared. This is why the world record has been broken so often in both sports because people are not afraid to fail as they discover how high they can vault or jump. I wish more people had that same attitude and played by the same rules.

You never know what you can do until you attempt to do it, but failing to attempt can simply be playing it safe because you don't want to knock down the bar, so to speak. I recently accepted some one-time opportunities to teach that kept me quite busy for an entire week. My first thought when asked to teach them was, "I am too busy to do all that." I accepted and taught a total of thirteen hours from Friday afternoon through Saturday evening. When I was done, I went home to bed, but I did it. What's more accurate is that God empowered me to do it.

What is God empowering you to do these days? In other words, how high can you jump? It's not about jumping, but about service, work, or some other practical expression of your faith. Do you really know how much you can do out or the potential you have?

MOST PEOPLE WHO SAY THEY CAN, DON'T

I often hear people quote the popular passage, "I can do all things through Christ who strengthens me" (Philippians 4:13, NKJV). When you stop to think of that verse, it is only a declaration of potential. Just because you *can* do something doesn't mean you *will* do it. If I say, "I *can* be a nice person," it doesn't mean I am exercising my potential. It just means I have the potential.

When someone quotes this verse to me, I am tempted to ask, "So what are you doing?" When I do ask, the question usually makes people uneasy, for that verse is sacred to many. When I challenge its relevance, it is tantamount to heresy. Let me ask you, however, since you cannot get mad at me face to face: If you can do all things through Christ, what are you doing? Where and when has that supernatural strength and power enabled you to jump higher than you thought?

After my thirteen-hour teaching ordeal, I was tired, but I still had energy to write and do some household chores. I cleared the bar of teaching that was set for me, and I am the better for it. What's more, the students I was able to teach are also the better for it, too.

Why not set the bar a little higher this week and see if you can clear it? Why not bless others, pray, write, study or read beyond what you thought possible and see whether it is possible? Why not choose to live in the truth of Philippians 4:13 and not just talk about it?

STUDY #28
WHAT ARE YOU DOING HERE?

In this chapter, let's look at a servant of God who was depressed and discouraged, or in the term of the day, he was "bummed out." His name was Elijah, and he took refuge in a cave after a difficult time in his life to sulk and complain. His way out of his funk was to hear the voice of the Lord. If you are "bummed out," that is your way out as well.

THE VOICE OF GOD

When Elijah was sulking in his cave, this is what the Lord said to him:

And the word of the Lord came to him: "What are you doing here, Elijah?" He replied, "I have been very zealous for the Lord God Almighty. The Israelites have rejected your covenant, broken down your altars, and put your prophets to death with the sword. I am the only one left, and now they are trying to kill me too." The Lord said, "Go out and stand on the mountain in the presence of the Lord, for the Lord is about to pass by." Then a great and powerful wind tore the mountains apart and shattered the rocks before the Lord, but the Lord was not in the wind. After the wind there was an earthquake, but the Lord was not in the earthquake. After the earthquake came a fire, but the Lord was not in the fire. And after the fire came a gentle whisper. When Elijah heard it, he pulled his cloak over his face and went out and stood at the mouth of the cave. Then a voice said to him, "What are you doing here, Elijah?" (1 Kings 19:9b-13).

When God asked Elijah what he was doing there, God wasn't looking for information. He already knew, but Elijah *didn't* know and that was the problem. Elijah was depressed because he was looking at the circumstances and not listening to the Lord.

Notice how God's voice came. It was not in the power of nature or the fire. Instead, the Lord spoke in a gentle whisper. You can't hear a gentle whisper if there is lots of other noise around you. Elijah had to block everything else out and listen to the voice that had led him up to that point in his life. It had never failed him and was not about to fail then.

WHAT ARE YOU DOING HERE?

Is the Lord asking you what he asked Elijah? Is he asking you why you are "here," wherever the here may be? If so, he knows why you are discouraged, and why you are delaying and hiding. He is not asking for His benefit but for yours! And you must do what Elijah did. You must learn to hear the voice of God, perhaps learning all over again. Perhaps Psalm 46:10-11 will help you: "Be still, and know that I am God; I will be exalted among the nations, I will be exalted in the earth." The Lord Almighty is with us; the God of Jacob is our fortress."

God is a great and effective communicator. If you aren't hearing, then the problem does not rest with Him. This week I encourage you to do what Elijah did: Get honest with yourself and God and then be still and listen. His desire is to speak to you. Is your heart set to listen and hear? I know God will reveal Himself to you and that His presence is the key to getting out of the cave you may be in.

STUDY #29
FEAR NOT!

In the previous chapter, we looked at the story in 1 Kings 19 when Elijah was depressed and discouraged in his prophetic work. He took refuge in a cave where he was hiding from the threats of Queen Jezebel. This story is like a situation in the life of the Apostle Paul. First, let's look a bit deeper into Elijah's story, and then move on to look at Paul.

FEAR

I did not point out in the last chapter that Elijah's problems started when he gave in to fear. He had just confronted and killed all the prophets of Baal as described in 1 Kings 18. When Jezebel threatened to kill him after that, however, he took off running:

> Now Ahab told Jezebel everything Elijah had done and how he had killed all the prophets with the sword. So Jezebel sent a messenger to Elijah to say, "May the gods deal with me, be it ever so severely, if by this time tomorrow I do not make your life like that of one of them." Elijah was afraid and ran for his life (1 Kings 19:1-3).

Imagine that! Elijah was afraid after his great victory over the false prophets, so he ran and ran. Once he stopped running, God spoke to him and sent him back to where he had come from to do the work that God had called him to do. It is interesting that the same thing happened to the Apostle Paul as we read in Acts 18:

> After this, Paul left Athens and went to Corinth. There he met a Jew named Aquila, a native of Pontus, who had recently come from Italy with his wife Priscilla, because Claudius had ordered all the Jews to leave Rome. Paul went to see them, and because he was a tentmaker as they were, he stayed and worked with them. Every Sabbath he reasoned in the synagogue, trying to persuade Jews and Greeks.
>
> When Silas and Timothy came from Macedonia, Paul devoted himself exclusively to preaching, testifying to the Jews that Jesus was the Christ. But when the Jews opposed Paul and became abusive, he shook out his clothes in protest and said to them, "Your blood be on your own heads! I am clear of my responsibility. From now on I will go to the Gentiles." Then Paul left the synagogue and went next door to the house of Titius Justus, a worshiper of God. Crispus, the synagogue ruler, and his entire household believed in the Lord; and many of the Corinthians who heard him believed and were baptized.
>
> One night the Lord spoke to Paul in a vision: "Do not be afraid; keep on speaking, do not be silent. For I am with you, and no one is going to attack and harm you, because I have many people in this city." So Paul stayed for a year and a half, teaching them the word of God (Acts 18:1-11).

FEAR NOT!

Paul had just come to Corinth from Athens where he had experienced very little ministry success. The Jews became abusive and opposed Paul, so he turned his efforts to work exclusively with the Gentiles. Do you see what the Lord told Paul? He told him not to be afraid. God doesn't tell someone *not* to be afraid unless that person is already afraid. Perhaps Paul was considering moving on from Corinth, just as Elijah had moved on to avoid an encounter with Jezebel. Despite the situation, the Lord told Paul to hold steady, for he had much work for him to do in Corinth.

Perhaps you are afraid and thinking of moving on from your current assignment? Maybe someone is opposing your work or your message. They could even be abusive and harsh. The word to you is the same as it was to Paul: Fear not! God is with you, and He will not allow you to be run off from the work He has called you to do. He can't stop you from running, however, if you give in to fear and anxiety. It should give you great comfort that Elijah and Paul were fearful; it should also encourage you that they may have wavered, but they never gave in to that fear—or God did not allow them to give in to it.

Are you facing opposition? Are you questioning your ability to fulfill your purpose? If you answer "yes" to either question, then I urge you to follow the example of these two great men and not surrender your life's work to the effects of fear. "Don't be afraid" is the word of the Lord to you this day, and may God strengthen you, as He did Elijah and Paul, for the great work that is yet ahead of you to accomplish.

STUDY #30
TOO LATE

I ran across a quote by Martin Luther King Jr. not too long ago that impacted me deeply. Before I share that quote, however, I want to share a passage from Isaiah that people recite and even sing to me regularly (it was put to music years ago). It is their life philosophy and approach to missions, creativity and action, and it reads like this in the NAS Version:

> He gives strength to the weary,
> And to him who lacks might He increases power.
> Though youths grow weary and tired,
> And vigorous young men stumble badly,
> *Yet those who wait for the Lord*
> Will gain new strength;
> They will mount up with wings like eagles,
> They will run and not get tired,
> They will walk and not become weary
> (Isaiah 40:30-31, emphasis added).

A CLOSER LOOK

The key phrase in that passage for many is "those who wait on the Lord." The implication is that if you are going to serve the Lord, you need to wait. There is only one problem with that interpretation and application. Everything else in that passage describes action (flying, running, and walking), not waiting. And why does God need to give strength to those who "wait"? I would propose that those who wait don't need any strength—patience maybe, but not strength.

For once, the NIV is more accurate in its translation of the word "wait," for the NIV states, "but those who *hope* in the Lord will renew their strength." Replace the word wait with hope in the passage from the NAS Bible quoted above, and you will see that there is a big difference between hoping and waiting. Most already have the waiting down pat. I want to be a person who hopes as I run, fly and walk, and I invite you to join me as we run together toward our purpose and creative fruitfulness.

THE QUOTE

Now for the quote from Martin Luther King's speech "Beyond Vietnam," delivered on April 4, 1967, in New York City. I will offer no commentary on his closing comments. I trust you to draw your own conclusions and make the necessary adjustments in your life and work to apply what he said:

We are now faced with the fact, my friends, that tomorrow is today. We are confronted with the fierce urgency of now. In this unfolding conundrum of life and history, there is such a thing as being too late. Procrastination is still the thief of time. Life often leaves us standing bare, naked, and dejected with a lost opportunity. The tide in the affairs of men does not remain at flood—it ebbs. We may cry out desperately for time to pause in her passage, but time is adamant to every plea and rushes on. Over the bleached bones and jumbled residues of numerous civilizations are written the pathetic words, "Too late." There is an invisible book of life that faithfully records our vigilance or our neglect. Omar Khayyam is right: "The moving finger writes, and having writ moves on."[3]

Where are you waiting and doing nothing, when you should be hoping and doing something?

STUDY #31
CRITICISM

Do you enjoy criticism? I don't know too many who do, but it can sometimes be an important part of your development. If you can't handle criticism and misunderstanding, then you won't go very far in your quest for purpose. Let's see if we can't learn some things about criticism that will make it a bit easier to accept the next time you encounter it.

SUCCESS BRINGS CRITICISM

When Gideon had won a great battle over the Midianites, some of his allies confronted him after his victory: "Now the Ephraimites asked Gideon, 'Why have you treated us like this? Why didn't you call us when you went to fight Midian?' And they criticized him sharply" (Judges 8:1). Gideon had fought on their behalf, but it did not prevent his friends from taking him to task.

This reminds me of another story later in the Bible when David was sharply criticized after his men's families were taken captive: "David was greatly distressed because the men were talking of stoning him; each one was bitter in spirit because of his sons and daughters" (1 Samuel 30:6a). After all David and Gideon had done, they had their critics, and you will have yours, too. With that in mind, you have three options of how to handle the inevitable criticism.

THREE STRATEGIES

First, you can become defensive, spending a lot of time and energy explaining why you did what you did. What's more, you can determine never to do much of anything again because the effort is too painful when it results in criticism. I would not recommend this first option.

Second, you can do what Gideon did:

> But he answered them, "What have I accomplished compared to you? Aren't the gleanings of Ephraim's grapes better than the full grape harvest of Abiezer? God gave Oreb and Zeeb, the Midianite leaders, into your hands. What was I able to do compared to you?" At this, their resentment against him subsided (Judges 8:2-3).

Gideon answered diplomatically and softly. He helped his critics see that their perspective was a bit skewed and that they were also an important part of what had just happened. Gideon showed restraint and wisdom, for he knew that leaders will be criticized. He deflected it and won his critics over with a gentle, non-defensive answer.

Third, you can do what David did: "But David found strength in the Lord his God" (1 Samuel 30:6b). David did not react or respond. He took some time to regain his perspective, and he did that by going to the Lord. The Lord spoke to David, and he returned to lead the very men who had threatened to stone him. What's more, he led them to victory.

I once thought that fear of failure was the greatest hindrance the people of God face. I now consider fear of criticism to be the number one obstacle to obedience. Since criticism is inevitable, it is vital that you develop strategies to deal with it and remain focused and purposeful. That is what Gideon and David did and if they did it, with God's help, you can, too.

STUDY #32
50 YEARS LATER AT 39,000 FEET

When I need inspiration or a word from God, I just need to get on a plane going somewhere, anywhere. I can't explain it, but it's a magical moment for me every time I fly, and I have logged 3.5 million miles since 1989! My love for air travel started when I was only ten years old, although it would be nine years later before I would get on a plane. Here's how it all began.

A FIFTY-YEAR-OLD MEMORY

My family never traveled anywhere. We never took a trip longer than 40 miles from our home and we never had a family holiday or vacation together. I remember playing in my back yard as a child and looking up at the airplanes flying overhead, wondering where they were going and why we were not going there. Then one day my life changed forever.

During some time off from work, my father told me that he was taking me somewhere, but it was a surprise. We got in our car and drove 32 miles to visit, not fly out of but just *visit*, the Greater Pittsburgh Airport. When we drove into the old airport (they have since built a new one), it had huge, elaborate fountains that changed colors at night. The airport itself had a variety of shops, great-tasting popcorn, a movie theater, a game arcade and an observation deck. This was probably in 1960.

Most of the planes landing and taking off were of the propeller variety, but I remember standing on that observation deck and watching them start up, take off and land. I was fascinated. We got there in the early evening and found out a jet plane was coming in from Chicago at 9 p.m., which was the time of the summer sunset. Dad said we could wait for the jet to come in and we did.

I will never, *ever* forget using the deck's binoculars to watch that TWA jet approach and land while there was still some daylight. I was absolutely spellbound and speechless. When we left after spending three hours there, I said to myself as a ten-year old boy, "I will be on one of those planes one day." I have fulfilled my vow repeatedly.

WHAT ARE YOUR MEMORIES?

That story is part of who I am. That visit helped shaped my life. Dad had no idea that our simple trip to the airport would make such an impact on my life. I cannot ever forget that 50-year-old memory, nor do I want to do so.

What experiences like I described have shaped your life? Are you being true to the impact of those events? If not, how can you reconnect with those things that helped make you the person you are today? Was it a concert, a family trip, a museum, summer job, visit to a hospital or movie? What was it about that event or experience that made it so special?

If you reflect on that event, you may discover some clues to your purpose that will help discover the riddle of your life purpose. Even if that memory was decades ago, it may not be too late to do something about what you had only once dreamed of doing. I would write more, but it's time for me to get on a plane, and you now know what a special event that is for me—and why.

STUDY #33
YOU DON'T HAVE TIME

There are two types of people in the world of productivity. There are those who say they don't have enough time, and they don't. Then there are those who say they don't have enough time, and they don't. Confused? You should be, for I have defined two separate groups with the identical phrase. What could I possibly mean by this? Ah, to find out, you will have to read on.

GROUP ONE

The first group doesn't get things done that they would like to do because they are waiting for conditions to be just right before they move forward. They are waiting to have the mortgage paid off, the children to be grown and gone, their retirement years to arrive, or to have a ton of money saved in the bank. Then there are others who are waiting for unrealistic chunks of time to become available before they even start on their goal or dream.

Someone once said to me, "I wish I could go off for about eight weeks and do nothing but write! Then I could get something done." I replied, "You don't know what you are asking. If you ever have eight free or uninterrupted weeks to do something, that means you have lost your job, broken your leg or are recovering from a heart attack!" The people in this group remind me of what the wisdom writer had to say: "Whoever watches the wind will not plant; whoever looks at the clouds will not reap" (Ecclesiastes 11:4).

Some of those in group one are perfectionists; others are fearful that they can't produce or do what they want, so they use the excuse that they don't have time to prevent them from ever starting or seriously planning.

GROUP TWO

Then there is group two who says they don't have time, and they are correct—they really don't! This group, including yours truly, usually tries to shoehorn four hours work into two hours. We can't say "no," so we tend to over-commit, believing that all things are possible for those who work hard and are called according to His purpose (a slight variation on Romans 8:28). Our to-do list is as long as our arm and even then, we feel like we are underachieving.

For group one, the solution is to be realistic. No one usually has huge blocks of uncommitted time, so they must learn to use what they have. This group must also deal with their unrealistic perfectionism, which says that only the perfect is good enough in every situation. This group would do well to heed the verses immediately following the verse mentioned above:

> As you do not know the path of the wind, or how the body is formed in a mother's womb, so you cannot understand the work of God, the Maker of all things. Sow your seed in the morning, and at evening let not your hands be idle, for you do not know which will succeed, whether this or that, or whether both will do equally well (Ecclesiastes 11:5-6).

For group two, the solution is also a dose of realism. If they are doing to do some of the things we want to do, they must stop doing some of the things they are currently doing. For example, there is only one way I could go back to school when I was 57 years old, and that was to stop traveling as much as I was. There are only 24 hours in a day and no matter how organized or committed I was, there are limitations. Where are those limits? I don't know; that's what you and I must find out. For group one, the answer to their challenge is a to-do list; the answer for group two is a *stop* to-do list.

I know which group I am in. Into which group do you fall? It would be good to find out and then take steps this week that will enable you to do some of the things that are important to you and that are in your heart to do. Discover why you don't have enough time and then find the proper mindset that will enable you to produce. The answer is either to be busier so you can use the time you have or to be less busy so you can use the time you have. Have fun figuring out which one applies to you.

STUDY #34
YOU ARE THE PROBLEM

You may be the greatest obstacle you face in your quest for purpose. It's not the economy, your education, how much money you have, or your age. The problem isn't any of those things. The problem is you. More specifically, it's the way you think.

What's more, you are probably trying to change yourself while holding on to old thought patterns, expecting different results while you think the same thoughts. You are seeking a personal transformation, focusing your energy on changing your habits, knowledge, spiritual disciplines or place of employment. If you are the problem, then wherever you go and whatever you do, you take the problem with you, along with your old thought habits. When that happens, even if you pray or read the Bible more, you won't see any difference in your life.

You need to change your mind if you are going to change yourself. Your old thinking won't take you to new places. It's that simple, but the process can be difficult.

SEND THEM HOME

In Matthew 14, Jesus had taught a large crowd of people in a remote place:

> As evening approached, the disciples came to him and said, "This is a remote place, and it's

already getting late. Send the crowds away, so they can go to the villages and buy themselves some food." Jesus replied, "They do not need to go away. You give them something to eat" (Matthew 14:15-16).

What was the problem here? Was it the lateness of the hour? Was it the lack of food that the disciples had? Was it that the crowd, in their zeal to follow Jesus, had not given enough thought about what they would eat?

The problem was this: The disciples' thinking too small and, consequently, they only saw one option available to them at that moment. They suggested that Jesus dismiss the meeting and send the people home. Jesus had another idea and that was to take what the disciples had, bless it and then feed the people with that. We know that this is what He did and the crowd of 5,000 plus women and children were fed with twelve baskets of leftovers. When you think too small, you do what the disciples did: you dismiss your opportunities because you don't think you have what it takes to seize the moment.

WE STILL CAN'T DO IT

Do you think the disciples learned their lesson? They did not! In the next chapter, we read how they complained to Jesus that there was no way they could feed a smaller crowd with the little they had (see Matthew 15:29-39). Jesus did the same thing He did in Matthew 14 and fed the crowd with the little food in their possession. The disciples were still stuck in their old patterns of thinking, and that limited their creativity and ability to solve the problem that was before them.

Are you any different than those disciples? The challenge isn't what you have and don't have. It's how you think about what you have and who you are. If you don't think you can, then you won't. What's more, you won't even try. If you think you can or if you think *God* can through and with you, then God will plant new ideas and thoughts in your mind, just like He did with the disciples when He said, "*You* give them something to eat."

Paul was clear about the importance of your thinking. If you are going to be transformed, you must do so by renewing your mind (see Romans 12:1-2). That won't happen, however, unless you take steps to make it happen. You must learn to be ruthless with your old thoughts that have gotten you nowhere and replace them with thoughts that can take you somewhere, thoughts full of faith and possibilities, not thoughts full of defeat and pessimism.

You must become aware of what you are thinking. Pay attention to your thoughts and listen to what you say. Be more conscious of how you are limiting yourself, or how you are limiting what God can do with the loaves and fishes in your possession. As you do, you will see the need to develop new thinking habits that will in turn transform your life into the victorious, glorious experience that intended for it to be.

STUDY #35
YOUR BOARD OF DIRECTORS

There are two statements in two different epistles that seem to contradict one another. The first statement is found in John's first epistle: "As for you, the anointing you received from him remains in you, and you do not need anyone to teach you. But as his anointing teaches you about all things and as that anointing is real, not counterfeit—just as it has taught you, remain in him" (1 John 2:27).

The second statement is found in Paul's letter to the Ephesians, in which Paul declared that teachers are numbered among the "big five" of ministry positions: "It was he who gave some to be apostles, some to be prophets, some to be evangelists, and some to be pastors and teachers" (Ephesians 4:11).

John wrote that we don't need a teacher, but Paul stated that teachers are critical to my development as a believer. Which one is correct? How can we resolve this contradiction? To find out, of course you must read on.

JOHN WAS RIGHT

John wrote his letter to some who had teachers telling them that Jesus was not the Christ. John labeled those teachers liars, telling the reader that they knew better. The "anointing" inside them taught them and bore witness that Jesus was indeed who He said He was. The presence of the Spirit in those believers also told them that those false teachers were in error. There were some things, according to John, that believers knew because the Spirit of truth resided in their hearts. They had no need for anyone to confirm or teach them.

One of those things believers "know," in my experience, is the truth about their purpose. No one can assign you a purpose. It is in you and, when you hear or see it, it rings true. I would say it is part of the "anointing" that John refers to, for it is something that is personal and directly assigned by the Lord Himself. That anointing not only allows you to know your purpose, but it also helps you fulfill your purpose. At the same time, your purpose increases your need for the Church and the "big five," which includes pastors and teachers. You can't stand alone once you find what only you can find and know your purpose.

PAUL WAS RIGHT TOO

As usual, there is no contradiction in the Bible on this point. There are some things you know, like your purpose, but there are other things you need to learn, like doctrine, right behavior and values. Your purpose sets you apart, but your need for coaches, mentors and teachers makes you part of a team, and that team is often found in the church. This doesn't mean that your purpose isn't relevant in the world of business, medicine or education. It does mean that you won't be as effective as you could be if you don't embrace those in the church who are assigned to instruct and guide you in the ways of God.

I hope you aren't waiting around for someone to tell you what your purpose is. That is something only you can find out and only you can recognize when it comes. At the same time, if you know your purpose, I hope you are a part of a team that can help equip and train you to be effective and relevant. Purpose is personal but how you express it is not, and that's where some miss it. Often no one can help you find your purpose, but many can help you fulfill it.

I have written in the past about your need for a personal board of directors, people who are living or dead who can train and teach you. Who is on your board of directors? Who inspires you to better performance? Who challenges you to grow and develop? Who helps clarify your values and then helps ensure that you live them? This would be a good time to first clarify your purpose and then to recognize and formalize your team of teachers and mentors who give your life direction. Make a list of who they are or make a list of who you would like them to be. Don't be confused, however, about their role. Only *you* can find your purpose but only *they* can help make it all that God wants it to be.

STUDY #36
I AM WHAT I AM, AND YOU ARE TOO

My weeks are almost always busy and full of purposeful activity, and recently I was reminded of something
that happened to me when I was in a busy season 30 years
ago. The lessons I learned then have served me well and I
thought I would share them with you in this chapter. What
are those lessons? I'm glad you asked, but to find out you
will have to read on.

SOMETHING HAS TO GO!

Twenty years ago, I was busy and involved in way
too many projects, or so I thought. I decided to spend
some time seeking the Lord to determine what I could and
should eliminate from my calendar and life. I was certain
that something had to go.

I prayed, listened, and kept a journal, yet nothing
happened. I got neither relief nor insight. Then one night I
had a dream. I don't remember the dream; I only remember
that a voice spoke to me in the dream and gave me a verse
from the Bible. I clearly heard someone in the dream men-
tion 1 Corinthians 15:10. I was not familiar with that verse
and had no idea what it said until I looked it up: "But by the
grace of God I am what I am, and His grace toward me did
not prove vain; but I labored even more than all of them,

yet not I, but the grace of God with me."

I continued to pray and journal, and God made the meaning clear to me. He wasn't going to send any less for me to do. He was going to send *more* but was also going to teach me how to handle more. He did, I have and the lessons I learned from that verse continue to bear fruit 30 years later.

THE LESSONS, PLEASE

Here's what I learned:

1. *By the grace of God, I am what I am.* People inquire regularly how I can do what I do. My standard is answer is that I stopped doing what I can't do so that I can do what I do best. Who made me a good administrator? God by His grace. Who did not create me to be a Sunday-morning pastor? God by His grace. Who made me with a love for sports and a good sense of humor? God by His grace. I decided back after the dream that if anyone had a problem with who I am, that's their problem. i cannot use that as an excuse for bad behavior or rudeness, but I can use it as a foundation upon which to live my life.

2. *His grace toward me did not prove vain.* This phrase showed me something remarkable. I can be the recipient of God's grace yet receive it in vain! You can talk about God's purpose, swim in God's purpose, write about it, and meditate on it. Yet your purpose is meant to make you productive in the will of God, nothing more, nothing less. I don't know how many days I have left to live, so I want to maximize them all. I am grateful for God's grace, and I want His grace to yield a return that will be pleasing to Him.

3. *I labored more than all of them.* God wants me to be a model of productivity and hard work. I am not to engage in any hard work, but labor that is related to my purpose and sphere of influence. From 2001 to 2008, I lived in Africa six months a year. During one of those years, I spent 22 nights on a plane flying somewhere. I did all that

because God wants me to work hard and produce! He has taught me both how to manage and have faith for time, and I know I can squeeze as much out of 24 hours as anyone. I do this not because I *must* but because I *choose* to. It is joy for me.

4. *Not I, but the grace of God with me.* My hard work and productivity cannot be a source of pride, nor can I impose my workload or expectations on someone else. It is what God has for me to do. I cooperate and partner with God. Yet if He wasn't with me, helping me every step of the way, I would not be able to do anything, as the psalmist reminds me: "Unless the Lord builds the house, its builders labor in vain. Unless the Lord watches over the city, the watchmen stand guard in vain. In vain you rise early and stay up late, toiling for food to eat—for he grants sleep to those he loves" (Psalm 127:1-2, NAS).

There you have my lessons learned from 1 Corinthians 15:10. Why don't you meditate on that verse and see how you can apply it to your current life situation? Do you feel like you're too busy? Are you as productive as you would like to be? Do you sense God's grace helping you daily? Have you learned to have faith for time? All these are important questions to consider until you find answers. I did, and the fruit of my insight from that verse has served me well and will continue to do so until my days are over.

STUDY #37
A BAD LEADER CAN TEACH YOU TO BE A GOOD LEADER

Have you ever been in a bad situation, one from which you could not escape or see any reason for being there? If you have been or are currently, then you are in good company, for King David was in a difficult relationship with King Saul. Yet God had put David in that scenario, for it was part of God's development plan for David as one of the greatest leaders the world has ever known. Let me explain.

A BAD LEADER

We can all agree on the fact that King Saul wasn't a good leader. He started strong, but he ended miserably. Saul and David began their relationship as close as father and son, but Saul quickly became David's nemesis. Even though David faithfully served Saul, Saul was increasingly envious of David and ultimately tried to kill David on three separate occasions. When those attempts failed, Saul spent years using the armies that should have been fighting the Philistines to hunt down David.

David suffered greatly during that time. Although David knew he was to be the next king, he had to endure persecution at the hand of the current king. Some of his followers urged David to take matters into his own hands and remove Saul, and others tried to act on his behalf. David resisted each temptation to dethrone Saul and punished those who tried, choosing rather to wait for God to put him on the throne rather than put himself there.

Why would God put David in such a position? Why did David suffer so long at the hands of a man that God had rejected as king? What was God doing during that time?

It's clear what God was doing. God was teaching David how to lead from a firsthand example of a bad leader. David learned more about leadership from Saul than from anyone else. What did he learn? He learned how not to lead! Can this be the answer to your current dilemma, which finds you far away from the fulfillment of a purpose that you understand and are ready to embrace?

TALK IS CHEAP

There are some who say, "If I was in charge, this would happen or that would not happen." That kind of talk sounds good. Even the leaders in Jesus' day said the same thing: "And you say, 'If we had lived in the days of our forefathers, we would not have taken part with them in shedding the blood of the prophets'" (Matthew 23:30).

The problem is that this talk is cheap. If you don't decide what kind of purposeful leader you will be *before* you have money or power, you are doomed to replicate the same miserable leadership style that you had to endure to become a leader yourself. You don't believe me? Read what Jesus said in response to those potential leaders: "Therefore I am sending you prophets and wise men and teachers. Some of them you will kill and crucify; others you will flog in your synagogues and pursue them from town to town." (Matthew 23:34).

God will eventually give you a chance to lead, just like He did David. David learned his lessons under Saul well and mapped out what kind of leader he was going to be while Saul was still pursuing him. What's even more important, David *became* that kind of leader. Jesus' contemporaries duplicated the same mistakes of the past because they didn't learn good leadership skills from their bad leaders. When they refused to learn, they were doomed to repeat history.

Why are you where you are right now? Why is your situation so tough? Part of the reason may be so that you will learn how *not* to lead when you finally get the chance. If people are being stingy with you, learn to be generous now. If no one expresses thanks to you now, remember how it feels and express gratitude when you are in charge.

If that's what God is teaching you, then you can embrace your current situation more enthusiastically because it simply part of your training. When you learn the lesson, God will move you on. Don't be guilty of saying today that things will be different when you are in charge, only to continue to model your leadership after the tyrant who oppressed you. Make a difference when you eventually have the chance to do so. When you do that, the hard lessons of those days will be well worth the price you paid to become the leader that God wants you to be.

STUDY #38
PURPOSE IS NOT ENOUGH

I regularly meet with people to help them find their life purpose, and I am always thrilled when I see the concept of purpose breakthrough in someone's thinking. I am working on some Internet options that will allow my purpose experience to impact even more people all over the world. There seems to be no ebb in people's desire to find and fulfill their purpose.

In the previous chapter, we looked at the prophet Daniel. Daniel was a success both as a prophet as an administrator in Babylon not only because of his gift and anointing, but also because he was faithful: "They could find no corruption in him [Daniel], because he was trustworthy and neither corrupt nor negligent" (Daniel 6:4). Daniel had skill but he also had integrity, and they go hand in hand if you are going to fulfill your God-given purpose.

A BIG MISTAKE

For all my emphasis and teaching on purpose, I find that many people make a crucial mistake in life, work and ministry. They believe the power of purpose or a creative idea is enough to ensure success. If you are serving God, however, you cannot overlook faithfulness, sowing, service and your heart attitude as important means through which you will succeed in your purpose.

There is a passage in Luke 16:10-12 that is critical to your life and purpose success:

> "Whoever can be trusted with very little can also be trusted with much, and whoever is dishonest with very little will also be dishonest with much. So if you have not been trustworthy in handling worldly wealth, who will trust you with true riches? And if you have not been trustworthy with someone else's property, who will give you property of your own?"

Here are some questions to consider from that passage:

1. *Are you faithful in little things?* This can include things like punctuality, follow-through on promises and all the other "little things" that can easily be overlooked in the busyness of life. As "small" as they are, Jesus said they are important, because if you are dishonest with those little things, you will act the same with the more important things.

2. *Are you faithful with money?* This would include giving something to the Lord's work when you have the chance, paying your bills on time, paying back money you borrow from others, and being free from greed and theft.

3. *Can you handle someone else's property as your own?* This includes being faithful with a business or church opportunity that belongs to another. For example, if you borrow something, you return it in better shape than you received it. If you quote someone, you give them credit.

A PARTNERSHIP

Yes, knowing your life purpose is vital to life success,

but so are integrity and stewardship. God is watching you, and He does not bless and promote solely based on potential or a good idea. God looks at the heart and He promotes anyone whose heart belongs to Him, which means those who will work and act like Jesus. You need purpose but it needs to partner with faithfulness if God is going to use you.

If we haven't already, maybe one day we will meet to talk about purpose. Don't be fooled, however, into thinking that purpose will guarantee your success. It's an important step in the process, but you cannot ignore Jesus' words in Luke 16 and expect to get very far in business or ministry. God is watching, and you had better make sure that your character matches the size of your purpose vision. Where God is concerned, purpose just isn't enough.

STUDY #39
DANIEL WAS WHAT HE DIDN'T EAT

In this chapter, I want to talk a bit about the life of Daniel. Both Daniel and Joseph are two "superheroes" in the Old Testament. They are almost too good to be true. They were faithful during temptation and loyal in the spite of persecution and trials. Both men are worthy of our study and emulation, but for now, we will focus only on Daniel.

MOST LIKELY TO SUCCEED

In some American high schools, graduating seniors designate one of their classmates whom they deem most likely to succeed in the future. Daniel didn't go to an American high school, but if he had, he would have been given that honor. Consider the kind of young people that King Nebuchadnezzar was looking for to serve in his kingdom: "Young men without any physical defect, handsome, showing aptitude for every kind of learning, well informed, quick to understand, and qualified to serve in the king's palace" (Daniel 1:4).

Since Daniel was chosen, we know that he qualified based on the listed criteria—smart and good-looking. Daniel had a bright future in his homeland of Judah, but God had other plans. While still a teenager, Daniel was whisked off to Babylon, selected for royal duty, and given a three-year crash course in Babylonian culture.

What was involved in this crash course? Daniel was sent to language school. He was assigned a new name. Beltheshezzar. which contained the name of one of the main Babylonian gods, Bel. He was then placed under the care of the chief of the eunuchs. Now I ask you: Why would Daniel be under this man unless they had made Daniel a eunuch himself? Here was a bright young man, with his whole future ahead of him, but suddenly he's living in a foreign land, called by the name of a foreign god, learning a strange new culture, and facing a future that didn't include a wife and family!

Despite all that, Daniel distinguished himself throughout his Babylonian career. He was a man of skill and efficiency and penned a book in the Bible that carries his name. What enabled this man to be so successful?

DANIEL WAS WHAT HE DIDN'T EAT

Daniel was a man of purpose, but he was also a man of values. When he first arrived in Babylon to become a royal official, he was also assigned royal rations that he was to eat. Daniel refused: "But Daniel resolved not to defile himself with the royal food and wine, and he asked the chief official for permission not to defile himself this way" (Daniel 1:8). If I am a teenager, having gone through all that Daniel had been through, the last thing I would have been concerned with was eating the local food. Daniel remembered the dietary laws of a Jew, however, and he determined to maintain a kosher diet even in Babylon. As a young man, Daniel knew what was important to him and he was determined to follow those values no matter what.

The most impressive thing about Daniel had such well-defined values at an early age. The second most impressive thing is that he was committed to follow them, even in a foreign land after his life had been turned upside down. Have you defined your values? If so, do you think you could follow them if you went through what Daniel went through? I'm not sure that I could.

Your assignment this week is to do some work to define your values. If they worked for Daniel, they will work for you. I have an article outlining how to do this in the Appendix entitled "How to Develop Your Governing Values." Spend 60 minutes giving thought and expression to what is important to you. Once you do, don't be content for those values only to exist on paper, but find a way to live them out in good times and in bad. Your values are essential to your quest for purpose, which we will discuss more in the chapter to follow.

STUDY #40
PETER'S PURPOSE PROFILE

God is often more comfortable with our humanity than we are. What I mean by this is that we let our failures and what we *can't* do keep us from doing what we *can* do. This wasn't the case with Peter. He made many mistakes, spoke out of turn and denied that he knew the Lord. Yet Peter was the one who stood up when the Holy Spirit fell at Pentecost and led thousands of people to Jesus. He was also one of the first Jews to go to the Gentiles and begin the revival that made it possible for you and me to serve the Lord. Yes, Peter was imperfect, but he was a purpose champion for God because he did not allow his frailty to stop him.

You can be a purpose champion too, but you must not allow your imperfections and mistakes to prevent you from fulfilling your purpose. I have encountered many people who are working to improve their weaknesses, not attempting anything for God until they or their circumstances improve. If you are doing that, you have adopted a flawed strategy. God is probably less concerned with your failures than you are. Are you more righteous than God? Can you have higher standards than God has? You're only human and not perfect or superhuman. Stop trying to be either. If Peter left a purpose legacy, so can you. If God is willing to work in and through you, then let Him.

AN IDENTITY RUT

When Jesus met Peter, his name wasn't Peter but rather Simon (see Mark 3:16). Jesus changed his name and today we don't refer to Peter as Saint Simon. Why do you think Jesus changed Peter's name? Perhaps Jesus wanted Peter to see himself differently. Jesus became not only Peter's Lord, but also his ministry coach. Coach Jesus decided that Peter needed a new perspective of who he was. From that point on, therefore, Peter was known as Peter, which translated means the rock.

Peter received a new identity, and Jesus expected him to walk in it. Every time someone said Peter's name, it was a reminder of who Peter was, not who he had been. Do you dwell on the past? Are you bogged down in an old image that others assigned to you and that you accepted? For many years, I was known as an administrator because that was what my job was. When I began to position myself as a speaker and consultant, some didn't recognize me and others opposed me, not willing or able to receive this new image and identity. I then had a choice: Was I going to revert to that old identify or forge ahead in my new one? I chose to forge ahead, yet some still refuse to accept me for who I am, clinging instead to who they knew me to be previously.

Are you stuck in an identity rut? Do some refer to you as Simon, while Jesus knows you as Peter? If that's the case, you have a choice to make. Whose report will you believe? Those who want to keep you as Simon, or Coach Jesus who wants to free you to be the person He knows you can be? That's an important but sometimes difficult choice to make. I pray you will have the courage to accept your Peter identity and shed your Simon label.

STUDY YOUR RESUME FOR CLUES

When Jesus met Simon Peter, he was working in his family business as a fisherman:

When Simon Peter saw this, he fell at Jesus' knees and said, "Go away from me, Lord; I am a sinful man!' For he and all his companions were astonished at the catch of fish they had taken, and so were James and John, the sons of Zebedee, Simon's partners. Then Jesus said to Simon, 'Don't be afraid; from now on you will catch men." So they pulled their boats up on shore, left everything and followed him (Luke 5:8-11).

Once again, we see that Simon Peter was hung up in his past, telling Jesus that he was sinful—as if Jesus didn't already know that already! When you spend time reminding God of your sins, do you really think He is interested? Do you think He has forgotten? That isn't the point, however, I want to make. Simon Peter was a fisherman. His job held a clue to his purpose. Jesus knew that Peter's purpose was like his employment, for Peter would become fishers of men, harvesting them for God's kingdom. On the one hand, Jesus was trying to set Peter free from his past, and on the other hand, Jesus was helping Peter see how part of his past was closely related to his future.

Does your employment history hold clues to your purpose? Don't be too quick to say "no." Do you have a resume? Study it and ask yourself some questions: What did I enjoy about that job? What did I hate? What was absent from the jobs I hated? Is there any common theme or activity among all your jobs? What feedback did you get during your job evaluations? Study the answers and see if there is any pattern that you can see.

LET'S REVIEW.

What did we see in Peter's life in this chapter that will help you with your own quest for purpose?

1. If God is willing to work in and through you,

let Him. Don't allow your mistakes or weaknesses derail your PurposeQuest.

2. Don't accept any other identify except the one that Jesus has for you.

3. Study your job history to see if it holds any clues to help you in your PurposeQuest.

STUDY #41
PURPOSE QUESTIONS

When I first began teaching about purpose, I made every effort to derive my material from the Bible. If I could not find purpose there, then I was not going to continue my quest to know more. That led me to develop what I called "purpose profiles" of individuals whose stories were included in the Bible's narratives. In this chapter, we begin a five-part series that examines the purposeful life of Nehemiah. Before you continue, you may want to read the book of Nehemiah.

In short, Nehemiah served the Persian king Artaxerxes, who ruled from 464-424 BC. In about 445 BC, Artaxerxes commissioned his servant Nehemiah to return and rebuild Jerusalem, the city of Nehemiah's fathers. This profile will study how Nehemiah got assigned to duty in Jerusalem and what he did once he was there. Of course, we will see that Nehemiah was a man of purpose or he could not have done the great work that he did.

The book of Nehemiah begins with Nehemiah asking some men who had just come from Jerusalem some questions: "In the month of Kislev in the twentieth year, while I was in the citadel of Susa, Hanani, one of my brothers, came from Judah with some other men, and I questioned them about the Jewish remnant that survived the exile, and also about Jerusalem (Nehemiah 1:1-2).

The point I want to make is that *you probably don't know your purpose because you don't ask enough questions.* I heard a motivational speaker say one time that quality questions lead to a quality life. What he meant was that you must seek the truth concerning who you are, and part of the seeking process is asking the right questions.

Nehemiah was interested in Jerusalem and its residents, even though he had never been there. One day a group of travelers from Jerusalem stirred his interest and Nehemiah asked a lot of questions. Their answers provoked him to prayer and thoughtful action. The rest is history.

When I first discovered my purpose, it was because I asked God, "If you didn't create me to start this business that failed, what *did* You create me to do?" That was a quality question. The Lord responded, "I made you to create order out of chaos!" That was a quality answer, the pursuit of which has led me to a quality life, one that enables me to do what I love all over the world. What questions are you currently asking? If quality questions lead to a quality life, do no questions lead to a nothing life? Do you continue to ask until you get an answer or some clarity on the matter?

Here are three good questions to ask as you seek your purpose. Work on these and there will be more in the chapters to come.

1. What would you do with your life if you had all the money you needed to live on?

2. What compliments have you regularly heard that may hold clues to your purpose?

3. What gives you the greatest joy?

There is no way to force the Lord to give you answers, and sometimes He does not respond because you are not ready to hear what He has to say. That's why it's so important to keep on asking, for sometimes God must prepare the ground of your heart to receive the purpose seeds. What's more, when you keep asking, you exercise faith that

God will reward you for your diligence. In the next chapter, we will continue our Nehemiah profile, but the lesson for you now is to ask and keep on asking good questions, trusting that you will obtain good answers.

STUDY #42
PURPOSE TEARS

In the previous chapter, we continued our purpose profile series with a lesson from the purposeful life of Nehemiah. The first point we made in the previous chapter was:

1. *You don't know your purpose because you don't ask enough questions—and keep on asking until you get an answer.*

Now, let's move on and focus on the second purpose lesson from Nehemiah's life.

WHAT MAKES YOU CRY?

When Nehemiah heard the answers to his questions to the visitors about the conditions in Jerusalem, he was deeply moved: "When I heard these things, I sat down and wept. For some days I mourned and fasted and prayed before the God of heaven" (Nehemiah 1:4-5).

Sometimes I substitute the word passion for purpose. Passion is a driving force that activates your creativity and will to do something. Tears of joy and sorrow often accompany that passion as you respond and make yourself vulnerable and available to a need that exists in the world. The first time I spoke about purpose, people in the room wept. I have seen hundreds more cry over the years. Tears and purpose seem to go together hand in hand.

In 1998, I was watching a television documentary about the suffering women in Afghanistan, and I began to cry. I remember asking, "Lord, why am I crying? I don't know anyone there but if you need someone to go to Afghanistan, I'm willing." Out of the blue in 2003, I received an invitation to go to Afghanistan from people I didn't even know. I went and it changed my life and the course of my ministry.

The second purpose point we can learn from Nehemiah is this: *2) Tears go together with purpose.* What makes you cry? I'm not referring to tears of sorrow when a loved one passes or when you receive bad news. Can you sit and listen to a certain type of music and cry? Do you cry during a sad movie? Cry with joy when someone is blessed? If you do, then ask the Lord questions like, "Why am I crying? What was touched in me that moved me to tears? What does it mean, Lord?" The answers may surprise you and hold clues to clarify your purpose. It certainly did for Nehemiah.

Purpose is not just a head thing; it's a heart thing. You need to involve your entire being as you search for purpose. That means you must pay attention to your feelings—it's called self-awareness—and seek reasons for what you are thinking *and* feeling. Purpose triggers joy and sorrow in your life; that's why those two emotions are so important in discovering your purpose. Don't ignore those two factors, and don't consider them signs of weakness. Instead, use them as launching points that will thrust you into the world of purpose where you will do what you are passionate about doing.

STUDY #43
PURPOSE CLARITY

I teach in a graduate-level organizational leadership program, and we focus on Nehemiah as a model leader. I am always surprised at the fresh, new insight the students regularly have into Nehemiah's story. I have found it to contain a treasure trove of material about purpose, and that will be our focus for this chapter.

WELL, I SORT OF, YOU KNOW, KIND OF LIKE . . .

Nehemiah prayed and fasted to clarify his passion and his life direction from it. After he sought the Lord, his big breakthrough came. One day he was serving the king who noticed that Nehemiah was sad. Let's read the rest in Nehemiah's own words:

> The king said to me, "What is it you want?" Then I prayed to the God of heaven, and I answered the king, "If it pleases the king and if your servant has found favor in his sight, let him send me to the city in Judah where my fathers are buried so that I can rebuild it." Then the king, with the queen sitting beside him, asked me, "How long will your journey take, and when will you get back?" It pleased the king to send me; so I set a time.
>
> I also said to him, "If it pleases the king, may I have letters to the governors of Trans-Euphrates,

so that they will provide me safe-conduct until I arrive in Judah? And may I have a letter to Asaph, keeper of the king's forest, so he will give me timber to make beams for the gates of the citadel by the temple and for the city wall and for the residence I will occupy?" And because the gracious hand of my God was upon me, the king granted my requests. So I went to the governors of Trans-Euphrates and gave them the king's letters. The king had also sent army officers and cavalry with me (Nehemiah 2:4-9).

The third point is that you must be able to state your purpose and goals with clarity and conviction. When the king asked Nehemiah what he wanted, Nehemiah had a ready answer. The king clearly understood, and could then either say "yes" or "no."

People often ask me questions to help clarify their purpose. At times, I ask them what they *think* their purpose is. It's then that I see just how hard it is for some people to talk about themselves. They will often say, "Well, I think my purpose is, sort of, like to help people. Yeah, that's it. And I probably, you know, encourage other people, but of course it's not me, it's the Lord."

Does that sound like clarity? You can't state your purpose and preface it with phrases like "I think," "probably," or "maybe." You either know your purpose or you don't. If you can't overcome the natural hesitancy that many have talking about themselves, you will always struggle to come up with a clear statement.

LET'S REVIEW

In this series so far, we have learned three purpose lessons from Nehemiah's profile. They are:

1. Most people don't know their purpose because they don't ask enough questions

2.   Tears often go hand in hand with purpose

3.   You must be able to state your purpose and goals with clarity and conviction.

In the next chapter, we will continue our Nehemiah profile. Before you go there, I want you to get your notebook, journal or a sheet of paper, and write down all the questions you can think of concerning your purpose. Write them all down, even if one question is, "What should I be asking?" I ask you to do this to focus your search by posing good questions. By doing so, you will have a better chance of obtaining good answers. Then, get comfortable not only talking about what you can't do, but also what you can do. Your objective is to be able to clearly answer anyone who asks, "What is your passion and purpose?"

STUDY #44
YOUR PURPOSE ENEMIES

In this chapter, let's continue the purpose profile of Nehemiah to see what we can learn to help each of us in our quest for purpose. Nehemiah faced a lot of opposition as soon as he began to rebuild Jerusalem, and that is the fourth point we can learn from Nehemiah's PurposeQuest: *You will always face opposition when you seek to fulfill your purpose—some of it from without, some from within.*

> When Sanballat heard that we were rebuilding the wall, he became angry and was greatly incensed. He ridiculed the Jews, and in the presence of his associates and the army of Samaria, he said, "What are those feeble Jews doing? Will they restore their wall? Will they offer sacrifices? Will they finish in a day? Can they bring the stones back to life from those heaps of rubble-burned as they are?" Tobiah the Ammonite, who was at his side, said, "What they are building—if even a fox climbed up on it, he would break down their wall of stones!" (Nehemiah 4:1-3).

That's how it is with people of purpose: your enemies don't show up until you get serious about doing God's will. Nehemiah wasn't the only one to face purposeful opposition. Joseph faced the enmity of his brothers when he shared his dreams with them. David incurred the wrath of Saul and the disinterest of his family after David was anointed king. Daniel was a faithful public servant in Babylon, but then his opponents conspired against him that ultimately had him sent to the lions' den.

Jesus didn't have an enemy in the world until He preached and healed on the Sabbath. After He did, there was a group of men dedicated to see Him die. Your enemies are signs that you are doing something *right*, not that you are doing something wrong. The Apostle Paul was a devoted Jew who then preached that Jesus was the Messiah. After that, old friends and even family became his enemies, some devoted to his assassination.

FEAR OF CRITICISM

I formerly considered the fear of failure as the most significant obstacle we face in fulfilling our purpose. I have changed my mind and now consider the fear of criticism as the greatest challenge. Sometimes our greatest source of criticism is from those who are closest to us. They become a purpose opponent because they think they know our purpose better than we do. They are threatened when we step out to do something, or they want to protect us from disappointment and hurt. Whatever their reason, those closest to us can be our most significant purpose obstacle because we fear their criticism.

As you seek to fulfill your purpose, where is your greatest source of external opposition? Is it from family, friends or associates? Identifying what you do that attracts the greatest opposition may give you a significant clue concerning your purpose. In the next chapter, we will talk about what attracts the most internal opposition from your own heart and mind, but for now, reflect on what you do that seems to rile people up the most. See if that insight can help you clarify your purpose and in the next chapter we will continue our look at Nehemiah.

STUDY #45
YOUR PURPOSE LEGACY

Let's finish up in this chapter with our purpose lessons from Nehemiah's narrative. In the previous chapter, we looked at the tendency for enemies to appear when you start to pursue and fulfill purpose. External opposition is serious, but it may not be the most serious obstacle where your purpose is concerned. It is the opposition from *within* that is often the most crippling. Fear, doubt and anxiety all serve to disable and render you useless where purpose is concerned.

That is our fifth point in Nehemiah's PurposeQuest: *Your purpose is bigger than anything you can accomplish by yourself.* You can read Nehemiah's own account of the internal opposition the people faced: "They were all trying to frighten us, thinking, 'Their hands will get too weak for the work, and it will not be completed.' [But I prayed,] 'Now strengthen my hands'" (Nehemiah 6:9).

Nehemiah's enemies threatened him, and the people who were with him were fearful. Nehemiah recognized what was going on and prayed for God to strengthen him. If you behold the need and then assess your ability, you will probably say to God, "I can't do this! I'm not smart or gifted enough. Help me, Lord!" When you clarify your purpose, you realize that you can't fulfill your purpose in your own strength.

When I went to Afghanistan in 2003, I said "no" to the invitation three times. I didn't have the time, money or energy to go, or so I thought. I should have recognized, however, that all those things only proved that it was God's will for me to go; I faced the internal opposition of fear, doubt and inadequacy. All those simply caused me to trust God more, so I went. What is it that causes you the greatest fear and doubt? Could that be telling you about your purpose?

PLAN YOUR OWN FUNERAL

Stephen Covey wrote the classic book, *The 7 Habits of Highly Effective People*. His second habit is "begin with the end in mind." To do that, Covey recommended that you write your own funeral eulogy today. His reasoning was that you must be doing today what it is that you want to be remembered for tomorrow. And that is the sixth point we can learn from Nehemiah's life is: *Your purpose is the legacy you want to leave behind.*

- "*Remember* me with favor, O my God, for all I have done for these people" (Nehemiah 5:19).

- "*Remember* me for this also, O my God, and show mercy to me according to your great love" (Nehemiah 13:22).

- "*Remember* me with favor, O my God" (Nehemiah 13:31, emphasis added).

I want to be remembered as a writer; therefore, I must write books. I want to be a man who was organized, which allowed him always to have time for people. That has caused me to study organizational skills and develop them. Do you get the point? Nehemiah prayed for God to remember Him. He desired his legacy to be more than a statue; he wanted to be remembered as one who did great things for God. God heard his prayer, for here we are, 2,500 years later, talking about Nehemiah's legacy. God did remember him!

What do you want to be remembered for? What positive comments do you want people to make at your funeral? The answers to those questions will provide additional insight into your purpose, for they help you identify what is truly important in your life.

LET'S WRAP IT UP

As we finish our Nehemiah profile, let's look at the points we learned by studying his life:

1. Many people don't know their purpose because they don't ask enough questions.

2. Tears often go hand in hand with purpose.

3. You must be able to state your purpose and goals with clarity and conviction.

4. You will always face opposition when you seek to fulfill your purpose.

5. Your purpose is bigger than anything you can accomplish by yourself.

6. Your purpose is the legacy you want to leave behind.

Those six points give you a lot to think about as you continue your PurposeQuest. Take those points and write down the insights you receive as you meditate on them. Don't take mental notes; the ink fades too quickly. Keep a purpose notebook or journal and record your thoughts, prayers and insights. As you do, you will develop your own purpose profile that will encourage and help guide others. If I can be of assistance, don't hesitate to write.

STUDY #46
YOUR SHADOW

There is a concept in the study of psychology called your shadow. It is an aspect of your personality of which you are unaware or choose to ignore, but that doesn't mean it isn't active. People may encounter your shadow side every time they meet you, traits like your sarcasm, competitiveness, need to control, fear, or need for attention. You can see why you tend to ignore those things, for they are in no way positive at all. Until you can bring those shadows into the light, they continue to operate and can damage your relationships, work and ministry.

Did you realize, however, that you also have a more shadow? It's the positive effects you leave whenever people have an encounter with you. While the psychological shadow is usually harmful, your spiritual shadow can be positive and leave a lasting impact for good. You are undoubtedly familiar with the Apostle Peter's negative shadow, his weakness that led him to deny the Lord after insisting he would *never* do that. You may not be as familiar with his positive shadow that is described in Acts 5:15: You can read about the Apostle Peter's positive shadow: "People brought the sick into the streets and laid them on beds and mats so that at least Peter's shadow might fall on some of them as he passed by."

This verse seems strange to some, but I take it to

heart and pray that the same dynamic will be present in my life: "Lord, help me recognize my negative shadow, so my positive one—all the encounters I underestimate or aren't even conscious of with others, can impact them for your purpose and glory!" Will you join in that prayer and then work to maximize every encounter you have with others for Him?

There is one other example of a positive shadow that is worthy of your attention. Look at this unusual story found later in Acts: "God did extraordinary miracles through Paul, so that even handkerchiefs and aprons that had touched him were taken to the sick, and their illnesses were cured and the evil spirits left them" (Acts 19:11-12). People went into Paul's workshop, took his work apron, allowed people to touch it and they were healed. That leads me to another prayer: "Lord, I want my work to touch people whether I am present or not. Use my life—my writing, speaking, teaching, and every other activity—in a way that brings healing to peoples' lives, whether physical, emotional or spiritual!"

My goal is to be a God-carrier wherever I go and in whatever I do. I want my shadow and my work—the extension of my purpose—to go with me, before me and remain after me so God can use them for His purpose. If that means I must make myself personally available for people to touch my shadow or my apron, so be it. My life is His and I will not worship at the altar of privacy if God wants me to go public. Join me in praying those two prayers and then develop your shadow and your work to such an extent that God can use them both to bring healing to hurting people who have been wounded by the negative shadow—their own and that of others.

STUDY #47
WHO ARE YOU?

I want to ask you a simple question and then help you come up with an answer because you will probably struggle with the answer. The question is, "Who are you?" When John the Baptist broke onto the Judean scene, he created quite a stir among all the people, especially the leadership. They immediately dispatched a delegation to ask that very question about his mission and purpose:

> Now this was John's testimony when the Jewish leaders in Jerusalem sent priests and Levites to ask him who he was. He did not fail to confess, but confessed freely, "I am not the Messiah." They asked him, "Then *who are you?* Are you Elijah?" He said, "I am not." "Are you the Prophet?" He answered, "No." Finally they said, *"Who are you? Give us an answer to take back to those who sent us. What do you say about yourself?"* John replied in the words of Isaiah the prophet, "I am the voice of one calling in the wilderness, 'Make straight the way for the Lord'" (John 1:19-23, emphasis added).

If John had not known his purpose, he could have easily succumbed to the definitions that were being presented. They tried to make him the Messiah, Elijah and the Prophet. John steadfastly refused to be seen or defined through the eyes of others but had a ready answer for those who challenged his work: He had come to prepare the way for the Lord. That statement represents his purpose, and it was biblical and practical. What's more, he had plenty of evidence to back it up, for people were streaming to visit and submit to his baptizing ministry.

Do you have the same kind of clarity that John had? What do you do when people press you for answers as to who you are, what you do best and what are you here to do? If you respond with vague generalities like, "I am here to do God's will" or "I exist to glorify God," then you will leave people no choice but to define you on their own. If you are afraid of purpose specificity, then you may be content to be known by others' labels. I am not.

In the coming days, spend some time rehearsing your answers to the questions: *Who are you? What do you say about yourself?* Take a long look at whether you have allowed others to answer those questions for you, or if you have answered those questions for yourself. Are your answers clear? Do they keep you focused when others are pressuring you to be someone else? Are they so clear that others can describe who you are on your behalf?

John the Baptist impacted Israel, not because he tried to be everything to everyone, or to fulfill others' expectations. He did so because he was a man of purpose. You will do well to follow in his footsteps and to have a ready answer for the world who wants to know who you are. God wants you to know as well, so armed with that knowledge, seek to be clear and consistent when confronted with the question, "Who are you?"

STUDY #48
A DEEP SLEEP

I once heard a pastor preach an excellent word on Jonah, and I had an insight into the concept of rest as he was speaking—even though rest was not the focus of his message. This chapter will focus on another aspect of Jonah's story—that he was asleep when the storm hit his escape ship:

> Then the Lord sent a great wind on the sea, and such a violent storm arose that the ship threatened to break up. All the sailors were afraid and each cried out to his own god. And they threw the cargo into the sea to lighten the ship. But Jonah had gone below deck, where he lay down and fell into a *deep sleep* (Jonah 1:4-5, emphasis added).

Jonah was trying to use sleep to hide from the Lord and the consequences of fleeing his purpose! Perhaps Jonah thought if he slept, he would not be conscious to any remorse or guilt over his rebellion. Jonah was in such a deep slumber that the captain of the ship had to awaken him to ask incredulously, "How can you sleep?" Perhaps Jesus, the Captain of your ship, is asking you the same question, *how can you sleep when:*

- you don't know how many more days you must fulfill your purpose?

- the God of the universe has given you an assignment only you can do?
- there are so many depending on you to fulfill your purpose?
- the world is dying and you have life?
- you have known for some time that God has given you something to do?

You can sleep or retreat into rest if you are scared or if you are in rebellion, like Jonah was. You can try to play the rest "trump card," seeing if God will exempt you from service, but I doubt it will work. Contrast the idea of rest with Paul's testimony of what it took for him to fulfill his purpose:

> Rather, as servants of God we commend ourselves in every way: in great endurance; in troubles, hardships and distresses; in beatings, imprisonments and riots; in hard work, *sleepless nights* and hunger; in purity, understanding, patience and kindness; in the Holy Spirit and in sincere love (2 Corinthians 6:4-5, emphasis added).

Dear friend, is there a storm brewing around you, but you are in a deep sleep? Is the Captain asking you how you can sleep at a time like this? Are you fatigued not from action, but from inaction, missing the joy and energy of God to propel you through whatever you are assigned to do? The good news is that God isn't angry, and He is willing to get you where you need to be, just like Jonah in the belly of the fish, once you throw yourself into the storm and trust God. Read Jonah's story again in Jonah 1 and 2 and then awaken from your place of rest to a place of action. I promise you God will give you all the rest you need, but first you must earn it. You cannot use that rest as an escape.

STUDY #49
THAT MEANS YOU

In John 14:12, Jesus made this astounding promise: "I tell you the truth, anyone who has faith in me will do what I have been doing. He will do even greater things than these, because I am going to the Father." In your opinion, what was the greatest thing that Jesus did? When I asked that, most people respond that it was when He raised the dead. If that's true, then what could be a greater work than raising a dead person? Raising more dead people? Clearing out a cemetery or hospital?

Many people don't think much about this verse in John 14 because they don't believe that they can surpass what Jesus did, regardless of what they consider to be His greatest works. If you think like that, however, then you miss a dynamic that could greatly help you be more productive.

Jesus did fabulous things but there were some things He *didn't* do. Jesus never opened an orphanage. He never wrote a book. As far as we know, He never founded a hospital or organized a group to go on a mission of mercy to a foreign land. He never started a business and never gave a large sum of money to a worthy cause. Why didn't He do those things? He didn't do them because He left those things for you and me to do.

YOUR GREATER WORKS

Therefore, if you believe in Jesus, and I assume

you do, why aren't you doing greater things than He did? Perhaps you have underestimated how important and powerful it would be to achieve the things that are in your heart today. You may also think that only a supernatural miracle would qualify as a greater work. Since you don't perform supernatural miracles, you assumed that John 14:12 was for someone else and you were exempt or disqualified from this tremendous promise.

I have faith in Jesus, and I want to do greater works. How about you? If you answer yes, then what will you do? Where can you apply your faith so that the results are miraculous? Maybe you will care for AIDS orphans or perhaps you will open a chain of businesses. You can create some educational innovation that will revolutionize the way children learn. You may invent some technique that will make life easier for others, enriching yourself in the process. Then you'll start foundations like Mr. Kellogg, Mr. Ford or Mr. Rockefeller that will fund humanitarian projects long after you're gone.

I hope you get my point. You may ask, "Who am I to think about doing those things?" If you believe in Jesus, the answer is, "Who are you *not* to think like that?" The question you must settle is whether John 14:12 only applies to a select few or to every believer, including you. If it's for you, then you have some work to do. The good news is that you're not alone if your work is coupled with faith. With faith, you are guaranteed that your results will be great, greater than you could ever imagine because God is with you.

THE SOMEONE IS YOU

What have you said *someone* ought to do? Could that someone be you? Write down in your journal what I call your elegant dream. You don't have to know how you will do it right now; you simply must know what it is. Let it flow out of you in its entirety. Once you write it out, study it. Let it become a part of your thinking every day and envision it as already a reality.

If there is something you can do to make that elegant dream a reality, what would it be? Do you need to go back to school? Do you need to have money to do achieve your elegant dream? Are you sure that's your greatest need? You may meet someone soon who can help you develop a plan or give you the money for this dream that could eventually qualify as a John 14:12 greater work. You must be able, however, to articulate that dream, before you can expect anyone to understand it and respond, and that may start with you accepting John 14:12 as possible not just for others but also for you. What are you waiting for? Get moving and have a great life proving the truth of that mind-boggling promise in John 14.

STUDY #50
TELL YOUR STORY

As I was preparing to teach a class, Psalm 105:2 caught my attention. It's a verse you are probably familiar with, but what struck me is that the verse is an exhortation for you (and me) to publish and broadcast! You may not see it like that but let me give you a little more background. First, here is the verse: "Let the redeemed of the Lord tell their story—those he redeemed from the hand of the foe" (Psalm 107:2).

Do you have a story? You probably do, for God has done great things for you just as He has for me. That is what's known as our testimony, and we are to tell it. One place to do so in church, but in today's modern church services, there is seldom time allowed to testify. That means you (and I) must find other ways to tell God's story as it has unfolded in our lives. That is where publishing, social media and the like come in. I don't often use social media for personal things, but I use it regularly to "publish" what God is showing me and what I am learning. I do my best every day to tell my story. What about you?

After I noticed Psalm 107:2, I did a little more research and discovered two interesting things in Scripture that go along with that verse from Psalms. One is in Deuteronomy 31:19: "Now write down this song and teach it to the Israelites and have them sing it, so that it may be a witness for me against them." God instructed Moses to write a song and teach it to Israel. The song's theme was to remind Israel of God's faithfulness in a day when they would go astray, but I had never noticed that God commanded Moses to be creative and write music. Do you have any music in you that needs to be written? That is another way of telling your story.

The second verse I found was in Joshua 18:4: "Appoint three men from each tribe. I will send them out to make a survey of the land and to write a description of it, according to the inheritance of each. Then they will return to me." God had commanded the spies who were sent out to submit a report in writing of what they saw in the Promised Land. Their story was not what God had done, but what God was going to do when they entered the Land He was giving them. Like the spies, part of your story is your faith vision of what is yet to come.

These verses provide three reasons to publish, write, and create: 1) to tell your story of what God has done for you; 2) to remind you and others of God's faithfulness; and 3) to report what you see pertaining to God's purpose and plan for you that is yet to be. What you have experienced in your life is not unique. There are others who are experiencing or will experience the same things. Your story can help them make it through their tough times or encourage them to overcome timidity so they can do God's will. If you have something that can help another, then God commands you to share it. That includes your story. Don't judge what you have as irrelevant; allow God to use it for His purpose and glory.

STUDY #51
THE IMPORTANCE OF YOUR PRESENCE

False humility involves denying your ability to do something well, so you don't appear to someone else as braggadocious or proud. While this appears spiritual to some, it dishonors the Lord who created you to do certain things well. It also causes you to minimize your strengths and purpose in your own mind and consequently in the minds of others.

The false humility usually leads to spiritual passivity, a lackadaisical attitude that says, "There should be no hurry or urgency in the things God has given me to do. I can wait." Worse yet is the attitude that your presence and purpose really doesn't contribute much, so whether you act is of little consequence—God will get His will done through someone else.

That, my friend, is a dangerous and erroneous attitude that deprives God's kingdom of your presence and the results that only you can produce. Your presence is essential to God's purpose, and I am thinking of two biblical examples to prove my point.

POINT ONE

One is found in 2 Kings 3:14 where Jehoshaphat had forged an alliance with wicked Ahab and they went to see counsel from Elisha the prophet. This is what Elisha said when they came into his presence: "As surely as the Lord Almighty lives, whom I serve, if I did not have respect for the presence of Jehoshaphat king of Judah, I would not pay any attention to you." Because of Jehoshaphat's presence, Elisha went on to prophesy what would happen when those kings went into battle. The point is: the word of the Lord would not have been released had Jehoshaphat not been personally present. There are also some things that will not occur unless you are present.

POINT TWO

The second is the almost humorous story of the sons of Sceva who were trying to cast out demons in Jesus' name. When those sons took on more than they could handle, this is what the demons said to them: "Jesus I know, and Paul I know about, but who are you?" (Acts 19:15b). The demonic world was aware of Paul and, when someone tried to do what only Paul and others like him had the authority to do, the demons turned on the sons of Sceva and beat them badly.

The point from that story is there are some things that only you can do and your presence in certain situations is necessary for God's work and will to be done. As you can see, point two is the same as point one.

CONCLUSION

The conclusion is that you must learn to take the power and importance of the purpose you carry seriously and not dismiss it lightly or treat it with a nonchalant attitude. There are people and situations waiting for you to show up to do what only you can do. When you think that your presence isn't important, the opportunity is lost. Yes, God will raise up someone else to do His will in the long run, but for today, you have work to do that only you can do and your presence is essential for that work to get done.

You may think, "I must wait on the Lord" and that's certainly important to do. Once you have found your purpose and see your divine assignment, however, the waiting is over. It's time to act and act you must, for you carry purpose power and authority that cannot be replicated or replaced. You need to change your thinking where false humility and passivity are concerned and act this minute to do the work that only you can do. Your presence is important. Now go find out where you are supposed to be and make the difference there that only you can make.

STUDY #52
PROPER PERSPECTIVE

I have written in the past about the practice of false humility and the harm it does to your purpose and productivity. When you deny the fact that you can do something well (false humility), you are talking yourself out of its importance and of your urgent need to do (or be) it more. While it seems spiritual to act with a lack of urgency, a passive attitude, and self-deprecation, it often hinders, and can even thwart, God's ability to use you. I ran across a well-known quote from the Scottish poet Robert Burns, which states:

> Oh that the gods
> The gift would gie us
> To see ourselves
> As others see us

We see the need to see ourselves as others see us when we are acting like jerks, which does happen from time to time. I contend, however, that the need to see ourselves as others see us is greater regarding our strengths and purpose, and not only in our sin and weakness.

MIGHTY WARRIOR

When the Lord appeared to Gideon in Judges 6, this is how He greeted him: "The Lord is with you, mighty warrior" (Judges 6:12). It's interesting that Gideon was *not* acting like a mighty warrior at the time; he was cowering in fear as he threshed wheat in a spot hidden from his enemies. Gideon went on to engage in false humility, telling the Lord: "'Pardon me, my lord,' Gideon replied, "but how can I save Israel? My clan is the weakest in Manasseh, and I am the least in my family'" (Judges 6:15).

You have probably reacted just as Gideon did, and I know I have, too.

God had something for Gideon to do that only he could do. God saw Gideon's potential when Gideon did not, either because he was unable or he refused. At this point, you may say, "Well, that was what God saw, and He knows everything." When God sees it (your giftedness, power, or potential), however, others do as well. Note later what someone said as they interpreted a dream another person had described as it pertained to Gideon:

> Gideon arrived just as a man was telling a friend his dream. "I had a dream," he was saying. "A round loaf of barley bread came tumbling into the Midianite camp. It struck the tent with such force that the tent overturned and collapsed." His friend responded, "This can be nothing other than the sword of Gideon son of Joash, the Israelite. God has given the Midianites and the whole camp into his hands" (Judges 7:13-14).

It wasn't just God who saw Gideon's potential; others saw it as well.

OTHERS SEE IT

There are times when you need to see yourself as others do when you are misbehaving. It is more important, however, that you see yourself as others see you in the power of your purpose. Paul wrote about this matter when he said: "For by the grace given me I say to every one of you: Do not think of yourself more highly than you ought, but rather think of yourself with sober judgment, in accordance with the faith God has distributed to each of you" (Romans 12:3). He warned not to think more highly of yourself than is appropriate, but he did not say you should accurately assess your strengths and gifts.

Where are you dismissing your power because you have been taught that it's the spiritual thing to do? Where has it caused you to be passive instead of aggressive in the revealed will of God for your life? Maybe you need to harken to prophetic words you have received, or seek out a trusted mentor, or listen to the encouragement that others are giving you. Whatever you need to do, I urge you to do it, stop acting like false humility is spiritual and get about the work of accurately assessing the importance and power that God has bestowed upon you for His purpose and glory.

HOW TO FOLLOW
JOHN W. STANKO

THE MONDAY MEMO

Every Sunday since 2001 I have written a *Monday Memo*
to discuss topics like purpose, creativity, and faith. You can
access it at:
http://www.stankomondaymemo.com

THE STANKO BIBLE STUDY

I have completed a verse-by-verse commentary on the
New Testament and I am not writing a weekly entry in the
Purpose Study Bible that examines the topics of purpose,
creativity, goal setting, time management, and faith as they
are found in the Old Testament. All these studies for both
the Old and New Testaments can be found at http://www.
stankobiblestudy.com.

ALL MY BOOKS

Are available for purchase on Amazon or through the
Urban Press website
http://www.urbanpress.us

MY FREE MOBILE APP

You can download the PurposeQuest app from https://subsplash.com/purposequestinternationa/app
I have many hours of video and
audio teaching there.

MY WEBSITE

http://www.purposequest.com
has all my video and audio teachings, plus some print
material, but doesn't have the daily devotional.

SOCIAL MEDIA

I publish daily material on all my social media outlets:
Facebook, Instagram, Twitter, LinkedIn, TikTok, and
YouTube. You can easily find and follow me on any of
those outlets by using my first and last name.

And of course, I am always available
through my email address:
johnstanko@gmail.com

ADDITIONAL TITLES BY JOHN W. STANKO

A Daily Dose of Proverbs

A Daily Taste of Proverbs

Changing the Way We Do Church

I Wrote This Book on Purpose

Life Is A Gold Mine: Can You Dig It?

Strictly Business

The Faith Files, Volume 1

The Faith Files, Volume 2

The Faith Files, Volume 3

The Leadership Walk

The Price of Leadership

Unlocking the Power of Your Creativity

Unlocking the Power of Your Productivity

Unlocking the Power of Your Purpose

Unlocking the Power of You

What Would Jesus Ask You Today?

Your Life Matters

Live the Word Commentary: Matthew

Live the Word Commentary: Mark

Live the Word Commentary: Luke

Live the Word Commentary: John

Live the Word Commentary: Acts

Live the Word Commentary: Romans

Live the Word Commentary: 1 & 2 Corinthians

Live the Word Commentary: Galatians, Ephesians, Philippians, Colossians, Philemon

Live the Word Commentary: 1 & 2 Thessalonians, 1 & 2 Timothy, and Titus

Live the Word Commentary: Hebrews

Live the Word Commentary: Revelation

Ediciones en Español

Cambiando la Manera de Hacer Iglesia

La Vida Es Una Mina De Oro: Te Atreves A Cavarla?

No Leas Estes Libro: (A Menos Que Quieras Convertirte E Un Mejor Líder)

Fuero lo Viejo, Adentro lo Nuevo

Gemas de Propósito

Ven a Adorarlo: Preparándonos para Emmanuel